Krabi Travel Destination, Thailand.

Tourism

Author
Henry Baek

Copyright Policy

Information-Source This Title is protected by Copyright Policy, any intention to reproduce, distribute and sales of this Title without the permission from the Title owner is strictly prohibited. Please when purchasing this Title, make sure that you obtain the necessary reference related to the purchase such as purchasing receipt. In accordance with this term, you are permitted to have access to this Title. Thanks for understanding and cooperation.

All-right reserved Information-Sourve Copyright 2021..

Published
By
Information-Source.
16192 Coastal Highway Lewes,
DE 19958. USA.

.

Table of Content

KRABI PROVINCE 1

INTRODUCTION 1

HISTORY OF KRABI TOWN 6

TRAVEL GUIDE 12

Family trip with kids 16

Unusual weekend 21

Visit the Observation Platform of the Temple Wat Tham Suea (the Tiger Cave Temple) 21

Observation Deck Tab Kak Hang Nak 22

Trip on a Horse to the Beautiful Places of Krabi 23

Kayak or Canoe Trips 24

Krabi Kart Center Racing Track 25

Rock Climbing 26

Culture: sights to visit 27

Attractions & nightlife 34

Cuisine & restaurants 40

Traditions & lifestyle 45

Shopping in Krabi 52

Tips for tourists 57

Best Things to Do in Krabi 60

Railay Beach - Krabi 61

Phra Nang Beach - Krabi 66

Railay West - Krabi 69

Railay East - Krabi 72

Tonsai Beach - Krabi 74

Koh Poda - Krabi 77

Krabi Emerald Pool 79

Koh Hong (Hong Island) in Krabi 82

Krabi Tiger Cave 85

Ko Phi Phi 89

Best Things to Do in Phi Phi Islands 91

Koh Phi Phi Leh & Maya Bay 91

Phi Phi Viewpoint 92

Bamboo Island in Phi Phi Archipelago 95

Viking Cave in Phi Phi Island 98

Diving in Phi Phi.. 100

Shark watching tours.. 100

Moo Dee Bay.. 104

Rock Climbing in Phi Phi 105

Captain Bob's Booze Cruise..................................... 109

Shipwrecked Boat Tour in Phi Phi............................ 111

Koh Tup and Koh Mor in Krabi 113

Krabi Hot Springs (Klong Thom) 115

Ao Luk Attractions, Krabi 118

Health and Safety *122*

Krabi Town Weather and When to Go........................... 124

Transportation.. *126*

Arriving and Departing... 126

Best airport and infrastructure 129

Getting Around 132

Things to Do in Krabi Town.. *135*

Day Trips 135

Events & Festivals 137

Hike to Huai To Waterfall (half day).................................. 139

Museums & Attractions 140

Off the Beaten Path 142

Scuba Diving.. 144

Shell Cemetery / Gastropod Fossil.................................... 152

Ko Phi Phi Quick Travel Guide for New Travelers........... 154

Understand 154

Krabi Province
Introduction

Located in the south of Thailand on the Andaman Sea, the province of Krabi has become one of the most popular tourist destinations in Thailand. With crystal clear waters, white sandy beaches, epic limestone karst peaks, and world class scuba diving and rock climbing, it's no surprise that visitors are flocking here in greater numbers every year. There's a lot to see and do here and many different places you can stay. Here's a short introduction to this beautiful corner of Thailand, highlighting some of the main areas you'll probably be interested in visiting:

Krabi Town

While there isn't much for tourists on offer in the town, chances are you'll end up here at some point by necessity. The airport is here and most long-distance buses stop here before

transferring you to one of the beach towns or islands. Should you end up choosing to spend a night here for logistical reasons, you could take a quick trip out to the Tiger Cave Temple. Scale all 1,237 steps to the top to admire the large gold Buddha statue and enjoy the panoramic views of Krabi. The name comes from what appear to be tiger paw prints in the stone.

Phi Phi Islands

A small archipelago of six islands, these have become a top destination in Thailand. This is thanks in large part to their appearance in the 2000 film *The Beach*, based on the cult classic backpacker novel. Every day, tons of tour boats pull up to Maya Bay where the film was shot. If you don't want to share the beach with hundreds of people, consider visiting very early or later on in the day. This is located on Ko Phi Phi Leh, smaller of the two main islands and uninhabited save for a few security guards and bird's nest harvesters.

The largest of the islands, Ko Phi Phi Don, is the only one that is populated, and this is where tourists stay as well. Much of the island was destroyed in a tsunami back in 2004, but redevelopment has been quick – perhaps too quick, according to some. The natural beauty of this island is its top draw, but many worry that this will be destroyed sooner than later if tourist numbers are not capped. Let's hope that a more sustainable tourism industry can develop here so that people can enjoy these stunning islands for generations to come.

Ko Lanta

Whereas Phi Phi may be known as somewhat of a party island, Ko Lanta is a much more chilled out place. Days here can be spent lounging on one of the island's many beaches, snorkeling, scuba diving, kayaking, fishing, or even trekking. The island is also home to a protected mangrove forest, waterfalls, caves, and a national park should you feel like doing some exploring. There are also plenty of options for yoga/meditation, Muay Thai, and even a few cooking classes. For a dose of culture, check out the Old Town, a mixture of Chinese merchants, Thai fishing families, and an ancient Sea Gypsy community. If you're visiting in March, be sure to take part in the Laanta Lanta Festival there, with food, games, and live music.

Ao Nang
This is the most accessible and most developed beach town in the province, and it's also where you can catch a long-tail boat to some of the other popular destinations. The beachfront road is full of hotels, shops, restaurants, bars, and travel agents, ensuring you don't ever have to go far. While the beach here isn't the best, there are plenty of excellent ones nearby that make for easy day-trips.

Rai Leh
Although it's located on the mainland, Rai Leh sure feels like an island. As it's surrounded by the ocean and mountains, it's only accessible by boat. From Ao Nang, it's a short 10-15 minute ride over depending on where you're staying.

This area features world-class rock climbing, boasting upwards of 700 bolted routes for all levels.

There are four main beaches that make up Rai Leh. Phra Nang Cave Beach features one of the most interesting sights in all of Krabi – a cave that local fishermen believe to be the home of a mythical sea princess. They make offerings to her to bring success and keep them from danger, and the offerings just so happen to be large, colorful, wooden phalluses. The other beaches are Rai Leh East, West, and Ton Sai.

History of Krabi Town

Pronounced 'Gra-bee', this small town located 814 kilometers from Bangkok is not a particularly attractive one in the conventional sense but a real rough diamond that tourists use as a base for visiting the major attractions and save time, hassle and money. Visitors take advantage of Krabi's fantastic night and day markets at various sites around the town and indulge in the magnificent views to be enjoyed from the river banks. Krabi today is the main port of entry to the province and indeed a bustling fishing port on the mouth of the Krabi River. It is finally developing and acquiring the reputation as a worldwide famous destination, and the history of Krabi Town is an ancient one...

Ancient Times

Krabi is a southern province on Thailand's Andaman seaboard with perhaps the country's oldest history of continued settlement. According to archaeological evidence, the area that is now called Krabi province had been a community since prehistoric period, yet there was no documentary evidence about this. After dating archaeological discoveries such as stone tools, ancient colored pictures, heads, pottery and skeletal remains found in the province's many cliffs and caves, it is thought that Krabi has been home to Homo Sapiens since the period 25,000-35,000 B.C. In recorded times it was called Ban Thai Samor, used a monkey as the town symbol and was one of twelve Thai royal cities. The first recorded history dates 1,200 A.D. when Krabi, or Ban Thai Samor, was tributary to the Kingdom of Ligor, a city on the Kra Peninsula's east coast better known today as Nakhon Si Thammarat.

200 Years Ago

At the start of the Rattanakosin period, about 200 years ago, when the Thai capital was finally settled at Bangkok, elephants roamed wild in the

Krabi area and an elephant kraal was established in Krabi by order of Jao Phraya Nakorn (Noi), the Rajah and Governor of Nakhon Si Thammarat, which was by then a part of the Thai Kingdom. He sent his vizier, the Phra Palad, to oversee his task which was to ensure a regular supply of elephants for the larger town. So many emigrated in the steps of the Phra Palad and settled down here that soon Krabi had a large community divided in three different boroughs: Pakasai, Klong Pon and Pak Lao.

In 1872
During King Chulalongkorn's (Rama V) reign (1868-1910), this land was called Pakasai sub-county under the direct jurisdiction of Nakhon Si Thammarat province. In 1872, King Chulalongkorn graciously elevated Pakasai sub-county to town status and called it Krabi, a word

that preserved in its meaning the monkey symbolism of the old standard. The town's provincial administration office was situated at Krabi-yai sub-county (in Muang district at present) and Krabi's first governor was Luang Tehp Sena. Krabi continued for a while to be a dependency of Nakhon Si Thammarat. This changed in 1875, when Krabi was raised to a fourth level town in the old system of Thai government in Bangkok. Administrators then reported directly to the central government in Bangkok, and Krabi's history as a unique entity, separate from the other provinces, began. In 1900 the governor moved the center of the province from Ban Talad Kao to its present location at the mouth of the Krabi River.

Krabi Name

As for the origins of the name Krabi, two legends co-exist. The first has it that villagers presented a large ancient sword ('krabi' in Thai) unearthed by chance to the governor. They also did the same when a smaller sword was found later. The governor regarded these two swords as sacred and auspicious, and as the provincial establishment was still in progress, he had them placed crossing each other in the cave named Khao Khanab Nam. This was the origin of the province's emblem: two crossed ancient swords in front of the Indian Ocean and the Phanom Bencha Mountain, with its 1397 meters above sea level the highest mountain of the province. According to the second legend, Krabi would derive from the name of the local tree Lumphi. The Malay and Chinese merchants pronounced it incorrectly Ka-lu-bi or Kho-lo-bi, which finally turned the name into Krabi.

Travel Guide

Sightseeing in Krabi what to see. Complete travel guide

Krabi is one of the most beautiful provinces of the Southern Thailand, which is located near the border with Malasia on the coast of Indian Ocean. This is the youngest tourist destination of Thailand. Within last years here have appeared comfortable hotels that offer world-class of service.

Krabi is a unique mix of wonderful beaches (cay and sand ones), crystal clean and warm water of Indian Ocean, majestic rocks that overtop water, various cays, tall coconut palms, fresh breeze from water, giant sea turtles, countless bright tropical fish that can be seen near the shore and, of course, beautiful tropical nature that is particularly beautiful during sunset.

However, nature is not the only sight of this place as in Krabi you can attend various places of interest – Tiger Cave Temple (a temple for meditation), Wat Klong Thom Museum (here you will see items found during excavations on the territory of the ancient temple), Tham Chao Le (it contains numerous rock drawings, stalactites, stalagmites), Tham Phet (the walls of this cave shine like diamonds in sunrays), Khao Phanom Bencha National Park that contains numerous caves and waterfalls, Than Bok Khorani national Park that is famous for its calcareous rocks and Emerald pool powered by hot underground waters, and cascade Ron Khlong Thom waterfall, the temperature of water in which reaches 40-50C.

The Island of Phi Phi Don enjoys great popularity among people who like to take a walk in picturesque places. One of its main attractions is the Monkey Beach - an incredibly beautiful stretch of coast, on which a large population of monkeys lives. For a relaxing holiday, this beach is unlikely to fit. Monkeys are very dexterous, so vacationers should carefully monitor their things. Tourists come here just to get to know these lovely animals, and this part of the coast attracts lovers of scuba diving.

Massive scenic spots and unique natural attractions can be seen while walking along the Ko Chiken Island. Its name is due to an unusual form. If you look at the island from a bird's eye view, it resembles a sitting chicken. On this island, there is absolutely no tourist infrastructure. Lovers of rest on little beaches, as well as those who have always dreamed of strolling through a pristine jungle, come here.

Krabi is famous for its healing thermal springs. It is possible to evaluate their unique features in the Nattavari District. Here is a wonderful thermal resort with swimming pools, spa rooms, massage parlors and a small hotel. Absolutely everyone can visit this thermal complex. For this it is not necessary to be a guest of a local hotel.

The island is known for its amazing reserves, one of the most unusual being the Shell Cemetery. The main attractions of these places are huge slabs of pressed shells that formed more than 40 million years ago. According to researchers, at that time, there was a marsh area on the territory of the present island which allowed mollusk sediments to develop. The thickness of some plates can go up to 40 centimeters. Their fragments are found throughout the beach. Locals from ancient shells, make very lovely souvenirs, which are sold in shops, right on the territory of the reserve.

In the island's capital Krabi Town, travelers can see the most emblematic monument that depicts a huge crab surrounded by smaller ones. This national symbol is very interesting. It is dedicated to the famous tower of Aesop's "Crab and his mother".

Family trip with kids

Family trip to Krabi with children. Ideas on where to go with your child

Family holidays on the Krabi Island should not be limited to beach activities alone. You should definitely visit the entertainment center, Poppy's Minigolf & Kebab Café with children. This theme park is stylized as a classical national village with a lot of entertainment for visitors. Original courts for playing mini-golf which will be awesome even for children, and also a beautiful café, are equipped in the park. Many tourists specially visit the park in the evening, when it is decorated with spectacular illumination.

Those who love water sports the most should spend a day at the Brill's Fishing & Water Park. This water park is special in that, in addition to traditional pools and water attractions on its territory, there is also a fish farm. Here popular breeds of fish which are then supplied to local restaurants are grown. Visitors of the farm will have the opportunity to personally fish in artificial ponds, and afterwards try fish dishes cooked at local restaurants. The water park also has excellent conditions for a breathtaking holiday; there are many colorful slides and attractions for children of different ages.

With older children, you can go to the Krabi Fun Park. This amusement park is sure to please those who have always dreamed of riding a bungee and love climbing trees. The park employs professional instructors who monitor the safety of visitors. Suitable attractions can also be found here, even for young children. The park is very beautiful and out of the ordinary. Accompanied by experienced instructors, visitors will be able to try the most incredible rides.

The Holiday Inn Krabi Kid's Club, is oriented towards kids. It is located on the territory of one of the largest hotels and is accessible to everyone. A significant part of the colorful attractions of this park is designed specifically for toddlers; they have a huge selection of swings and carousels, colorful slides and gymnastic attractions for them. For children are also equipped special game rooms, and a team of animators in the park.

Krabi Kart Speedway is a great place for a vacation with teenagers. It is famous for its first-class equipment and a wide range of routes of different levels. It will be exceptional to spend time here even for those who have never been fond of racing in miniature cars. The carting center is outdoors and borders with a beautiful forest park area. After the entertainment center, guests can stroll through the picturesque surroundings or relax in a cozy cafe.

Catfish Farm is the perfect place to relax with children. This original farm for growing catfish is located near the popular Khlong Muang beach. From an ordinary fish farm, it has long turned into a mini zoo, in which colorful parrots, monkeys, little goats and other friendly representatives of the animal world live. Absolutely all the animals in this mini-zoo can be petted, and some can even be carried. A tour of the farm will give a lot of impressions to both children and adults.

The main inhabitants of the Ao Nang Snake Show center are snakes. Every day in the center, mesmerizing excursions and exciting performances with the participation of trained snakes are conducted. Some snakes are completely harmless, and visitors are allowed to hold them and make memorable photos. The bite of other snakes is deadly, only the specially trained staff of the center can come in contact with them.

Unusual weekend

How to spend top weekend in Krabi - ideas on extraordinary attractions and sites

Visit the Observation Platform of the Temple Wat Tham Suea (the Tiger Cave Temple)

There is a cave in the forest 3 kilometers north of Krabi. The Wat Tham Suea Buddhist temple is located in it. You can enter it for free. But it is better to leave 20 baht in the donation box. There is a viewing platform on the second floor. You will go up to it by a staircase consisting of 1237 steps. Some of them are located almost vertically. Therefore, the ascent will be quite difficult.

It's hot here. Therefore, do not forget to bring a bottle of water, which you will drink while relaxing on the equipped platforms. You will see the statue of Buddha and admire the panorama of rubber thickets, mountain ranges, and beaches with snow-white sand all the way. It is better to start climbing to the observation platform early in the morning. There is no extreme heat and monkeys that will interfere with you after 10 o'clock in the morning, getting into your bag or pockets.

Observation Deck Tab Kak Hang Nak

There is a mountain range Tab Kak Hang Nak on the coast in the western part of Krabi. The observation platform with the same name is located at an altitude of 500 meters above sea level here. You can climb it on a 5-kilometer trail. The road up the mountain takes 3 hours. You will descend from it in just 1.5 hours. You will admire the amazing landscape when you get to the site. It is especially beautiful at dawn and sunset. There is also a small glade and a fire pit near it. You will be able to put up a tent and spend the night there. You must make the ascent before 4 pm in this case. Don't forget to bring water and food.

Trip on a Horse to the Beautiful Places of Krabi

You should rent a horse to enjoy the beauty of Krabi. You should contact the local equestrian club for this. It is located between the Circle Inn Ao Nam Mao Beach and Shelly Beach. You will take a fascinating walk along the coast or around the town while sitting on a horse. If you choose the first option of the trip you will pay 800 baht for renting a horse. If you prefer the second option the price will depend on the route of the trip and its duration. But the most beautiful views are waiting for you at sunset.

You will hire a guide if necessary. He will show you the most interesting places in Krabi. The guide will also tell you about local attractions, traditions, and historical events. The staff of the equestrian club will also offer you to go on a tour. It will last for half a day. The tour costs 2 thousand baht. You will visit a beach, a suburb, and a farm where fish are bred.

Kayak or Canoe Trips

You should explore the most picturesque places of Krabi by taking a trip on the water. You can rent a kayak or canoe on any of the town's beaches or from travel agencies. They are opened in hotels located on the coast. You will pay 100-300 baht for 1 hour of rent. You can make a trip on the canals in the Than Bok Khorani National Park.

You will see mangroves and several caves once you are here. Ancient paintings have been preserved on caves' walls. You will also reach Ao Phang Nga National Park. Panak Island especially deserves your attention among its islands. There are 9 beautiful lagoons on it. You will also visit the picturesque lagoon. It is located in the central part of Hong Island. Rocks surround it. You will not be able to reach it on foot because of this.

Krabi Kart Center Racing Track

You should visit the Krabi Kart center. There is a race track here. It is open from 9:30 to 19:00 every day. You will rent a single or double kart and choose the route based on your experience of karting. There are straight sections of the road. They will suit you if you are a novice racer. There are also winding trails. They will suit you if you are a professional. You will pay from 800 to 1200 baht. You will get behind the wheel of the kart and make a race on the track, developing a speed of 70-90 kilometers per hour. But you will put on a helmet and gloves before that. You will not be allowed on the track without such equipment. You can also practice paintball in Krabi Kart. You will pay 800 baht for 50 balls of paint.

Rock Climbing

There are many high cliffs in Krabi. Professional instructors work here. If you hire one of them you will be trained for 3-5 days. He will show you how to use safety equipment and tie knots. The instructor will prepare you for an independent route on the rock. You will choose it if you purchase a travel guide. Pay attention to the rocks of Tonsai Beach. You will get here by boat or a fast boat. You will pay from 100 to 150 baht. You will apply your climbing skills here.

Culture: sights to visit

Culture of Krabi. Places to visit - old town, temples, theaters, museums and palaces
Besides beautiful beaches and clear sea, Krabi has to offer its guests a lot of interesting places to walk. You should definitely include in the excursion a visit to natural attractions, ancient caves and historical sites. The Tiger Cave Temple

is considered an important symbol of Krabi. It has received its name because of the unusual shape of the stone located at the entrance. With its shape it resembles a tiger's claw; the cave is located at the foot of a high hill.

Not far from it the stairway is located, on which everyone can climb to the top of the hill and appreciate the panorama of the island. The stairway has 1237 steps, so climbing will be a good exercise for the curious traveler. On the island archaeological excavations were held for many years. During that time scientists have found a number of unique artifacts. You can see those archaeological findings in the Wat Klong Thom Museum; among exhibits presented here, there are collections of glassware, antique coins and jewelry.

On the grounds of a beautiful rainforest, beyond the mountains, there is Tham Chao Le cave. In addition to the incredible beauty of stalactites and stalagmites, tour participants will be able to see rock carvings dating back thousands of years. It is always worth a visit the 'diamond' Tham Phet cave. Interior walls of the cave are covered with special stones that shine in the sun like real diamonds. This cave can be called the most unusual and beautiful on the island.

A famous tourist attraction is the Than Bok Khorani park. The territory of the national park also houses some beautiful caves and magnificent Emerald Pool. The pool has a natural origin, it is filled with water of beautiful green hue. It changes color depending on the time of day. To enjoy the emerald glow, you need to come to the pool at dawn. There is also the blue lake in the park. It is quite shallow, so you can see a geyser at the bottom. Among other natural attractions, the Ron Khlong Thom waterfall should be mentioned. Here the water temperature reaches about 50 degrees Celsius; the slope of the waterfall is specially equipped to take water treatments.

Despite the fact that the name of the city has nothing to do with crabs, walking on it, you can find a magnificent sculpture depicting three crustaceans worshiping another huge crab. It was built inspired by Aesop's fable "The Crab and His Mom." Today, the sculpture is considered a symbol of the city, its image can be seen on postcards and postage stamps. It is believed that rubbing a coin on a monument brings good luck in all things. And this is true - be sure to perform the above actions to check. The city has some other interesting sculptures. The most famous after the aforementioned one is a memorial in honor of the tsunami victims.

Several beautiful religious monuments can be found in the city. First of all, it is worth noting the Buddhist temple Wat Kaew Ko Wararam striking with its snow-white splendor. A beautiful snow-white staircase with golden railings with sculptures depicting nagas leads to the shrine, and inside you can find a wonderful statue of Buddha seated in the lotus position. It is also worth taking a stroll through the picturesque courtyard where sculptures of elephants and tigers can be seen. From afar, the building looks very majestic, attracting every guest of the city. Even more impressive views can be enjoyed from the stairs. As for its construction, the building was erected in 1887 on the site of a former monastery with several monks cells.

Another Buddhist temple called Kwam Im is located in close proximity to the Tiger Cave Temple. A typical Buddhist shrine with a corresponding interior and exterior - this is what appears before the eyes of visitors. No less remarkable is Ao Nang Mosque, not least because it is the only Muslim shrine in Krabi. It is beautiful in terms of architecture, which attracts any tourist. The building is beautifully illuminated at night, therefore, in order to get an unforgettable aesthetic pleasure, it's recommended to visit the mosque after dusk. Not only Muslims can get inside (as is typical for Islamic temples), so tourists can admire not only the magnificent exterior of the shrine but also its elegant interior.

The city also has a Catholic church - St Agnes Catholic Church. The church is not large but decorated in quite an unusual style - both outside and inside. Such a unique church cannot be found anywhere else - and this is precisely what attracts many tourists. Another peculiarity is that one needs to remove shoes before entering - this is the tradition. Nearby is the wonderful park Shangri-la Crag striking with its picturesque spaces, which is a great place to walk. Grotto of Our Lady of Lourdes can be visited in the same area. To enjoy the magnificent views of Krabi and its surroundings, be sure to climb Khao Ngon Nak. However, it should be borne in mind that the climb would be quite difficult and require appropriate equipment (comfortable shoes) - the path to the observation platform lies through the jungle.

Attractions & nightlife

City break in Krabi. Active leisure ideas for Krabi - attractions, recreation and nightlife
Krabi is a resort attractive for those who prefer to spend vacation on a beach. There is absolutely everything you need for fun and exciting pastime: clean white beaches, beautiful places for scuba diving, colorful nightlife and beach bars, as well as magnificent nature which will help to escape city life. The most attractive destination for divers is Ao Nang bay. The beauty of the underwater world here is mesmerizing; the bay is a perfect place for beginners in diving. Several rental centers of sports equipment are located on the beach, so travelers don't have to take the whole stuff with them. Experienced divers can explore the nearby islands of Po Dha, Hat Rai Le and Tup, as the coastal zone there also has a rich underwater world.

The most beautiful and popular beach resort is Phra Nang, whose only drawback is a huge number of tourists. The beach is perfectly equipped for your comfort. Fans of active holidays would also like it, as the beach area is equipped with a variety of sports facilities, including those for children. Tourists, who want to be away from crowds on the coast, are recommended to go to the nearby Tup island. The beach there is no less spectacular, however, in comparison with the crowded beaches of Krabi, it has a quiet and relaxing atmosphere.

Several hot springs are located near Hat Noppharat beach, so the water is very warm all year round. The beach is perfect for a family vacation, it is located next to several attractive restaurants and cafes. Those who travel with family would be interested in visiting Tree Top

Adventure park that is located right in the middle of the rainforest. You can just walk around and appreciate scenic natural attractions or try to force the most incredible rides. Both young visitors and their parents will be able to choose the right place for entertainment.

Fans of spa treatments are recommended to visit the Kantawan center, which will please with plenty of massage and cosmetician's rooms. Be sure to try the diversity of Krabi's nightlife. The most popular clubs and discos are located near the coast. The Mermaids invites guests to participate in a colorful party. Fans of exotic cocktails and music would like the Traveller bar. Tourists searching for souvenirs are recommended to visit the National Park that hosts a huge number of interesting stalls and craft shops.

Safaris are quite popular in Krabi, and besides diving, sunbathing and swimming in the Andaman Sea, other water activities such as kayaking, fishing, boating, and yachting are equally enjoyable. Travelers will certainly appreciate hiking in the mountains. Beginners will be able to learn climbing under the clear guidance of an instructor, and more experienced climbers can find that this is one of the best places on the planet for their favorite pastime. Mother nature has created all the conditions for that. You can take tours from Tex Rock Climbing or visit Hollow Mountain Extreme Adventure Park to have a good time. Bungee jumping is available here as well.

Another great place to spend time actively is Zipline Adventure by Aonang Fiore Resort, where you can climb a rope course. However, the same can be found in Krabi Fun Park, which promises an equally exciting experience. Karting is another popular entertainment in Krabi, and you can try it out in Krabi Kart Speedway. Those who wish to improve their accuracy should go to Krabi Shooting Range - especially if you're traveling with friends, as this is one of the best activities for a noisy company.

Those who've loved Thai cuisine so much that now want to learn to cook like they do in Thailand are welcome in Thai Charm Cooking School. This is an amazing and exciting experience, which leaves only pleasant memories. Rick's Bar is a great place for those who want to play billiards, darts, as well as have a glass or two of some strong drink. Be sure to visit Aonang Snake House and watch amazing snake shows that are organized here for visitors.

Participants not only show what their snakes are capable of but also tell interesting facts about the inhabitants. Another mini-zoo is worth visiting - namely, Catfish Farm, where visitors can see parrots, monkeys, crocodiles, as well as lots of fish, including catfish, small aquarium fish, carps.

Of great interest in Krabi are bars where one can spend free time after dusk. Thus, for those who want to dance all night long, the best option would be Chang Bar, those wishing to share a nice atmosphere with friends while listening to local musicians should consider Roots Rock Reggae Bar, and fans of noisy places should never ignore Chang Bar. By the way, here you can not only drink but also smoke a hookah. Old West Bar is attractive for its special cozy atmosphere, quality music plays and excellent drinks are served here for guests. Tew Lay Bar can be called the most original bar in Krabi. You can find it on a tree right on the beach. Well, those who want to try the best cocktails in town should be recommended to visit Get Rad's.

Cuisine & restaurants

Cuisine of Krabi for gourmets. Places for dinner best restaurants

Local cuisine has an abundance of original dishes. Those who prefer hot and spicy food would enjoy a vacation in restaurants of Krabi. The abundance of spices and herbs is one of the main distinguishing features of the national cuisine. For many travelers, accustomed to European cuisine, this feature can be a real problem. The best salvation for those who struggle with spicy dishes is rice. It forms the basis of the local cuisine, that's why it is almost always on the table.

Rice becomes the basis of interesting side dishes for meat, as well as for original independent dishes. In restaurants visitors are offered two kinds of rice: 'khao suay', that means crisp rice eaten with a spoon, and 'khao nieo' that stands for glutinous rice, which is usually eaten with fingers. One of the most popular dishes among travelers is khao phat, fried rice, which can be complemented with a wide variety of ingredients. Pieces of vegetables or meat, fish or vegetables - those are components, because of which khao phat has thousands of variations.

Another important component of the national cuisine is noodles. Depending on your preferences, you can enjoy the most tender rice noodles or to order appetizing egg noodles. Those who prefer energy food would find for themselves khqetthieo sen yai, thick and hearty noodles. As well as rice, noodles may be served in addition to meat or fish dishes, as well as a separate dish. You are sure to taste noodles with the naam broth, as well as noodles with fish or meat meatballs, named 'luuk jin.'

Exotic fruits remain main desserts. It is worth noting that local people don't pay special interest to sweets. However, a sweet tooth won't be upset, as it is possible to taste some interesting national desserts. The sweet meringue, foy thong, which can be ordered at local cafes or bought on the market, is widespread. Various puddings are cooked from rice and vegetables; mince pies with various fruit fillings are ubiquitous. The island also has some fashionable eating places that would surprise visitors with an abundance of exotic dishes and attractive outdoor cafes that budget travelers would like.

The island offers restaurants of various price categories, which suit both budget travelers and demanding gourmets who never save on tasting refined delicacies. Widely spread on the island are Thai restaurants where guests can taste exquisite seafood dishes. One of the best in this category is Thailandia. This restaurant is located in the capital and is considered one of the most expensive on the island, it serves many rare seafood specialties. For cooking here they use authentic Thai spices so the taste they get is simply unique.

Viva da Renato specializing in Italian cuisine invites its guests to enjoy a huge selection of pasta, risotto and ravioli, traditional lasagna and the best Italian wines. Many people come to this restaurant specifically to enjoy their favorite Italian desserts, which are distinguished by a very beautiful and original presentation.

The best place to try seafood is Ao Nang Beach, a continuous series of small restaurants, most of which have very affordable prices. Walking along the 450-meter-long beach, you can watch how chefs in small cafes and restaurants prepare popular dishes right in front of visitors. On the coast, one can find the famous La Casa restaurant where the seafood is used to prepare popular Thai dishes. Widespread Italian dishes are present on the menu as well.

In the same area is the popular Chinese restaurant Ao Nang Cusine, which is very popular with supporters of healthy food. Only the best quality products are used here for cooking. All the dishes are prepared with minimal use of salt and oil, special spices make food taste truly fantastic.

Lae Lay Grill is a very original restaurant with a menu mainly based on seafood. All seafood is grilled, guests can taste the refined sea bass, crabs and squid, as well as dozens of shrimp. All the dishes here are prepared from the freshest seafood caught by local fishermen.

Traditions & lifestyle

Colors of Krabi traditions, festivals, mentality and lifestyle

Locals feature a friendly and welcoming attitude to people of another culture; foreigners are treated with interest and respect. Residents of Krabi are very laid back and relaxed people; violent emotions and loud tone of voice are considered signs of mauvais tone. Be sure to communicate with locals in calm voice; they don't tolerate any haste during a conversation, so don't force and proceed to discussing serious issues from the very first minutes of communication.

The local culture prohibits any contact during conversations, even the customary handshake is not accepted. In order to greet the person, just put your hands on the chest and lean forward a bit; this form of greeting is appropriate for both men and women. If you had accidentally touched passer in public place or institution, be sure to stop and apologize. Going to visit a new friend, it is worth considering a few simple rules. When entering a private home, be sure to take off your shoes; you can just leave it at the door. During the conversation, in any case, don't cross your hands or feet, such a posture will be regarded as disrespect and unwillingness to communicate. It is usual to pay visits with gifts; modest souvenirs for hosts would be a great solution.

The cultural life of Krabi is full of interesting holidays and festivals. One of the most interesting national celebrations is Loy Krathong festival, the All Souls' Day. They celebrate it according to the lunar calendar, so every year the date of the holiday changes. Despite the fact that the event is quite serious, it is accompanied by a number of interesting rituals, which attract lots of observing tourists.

On the eve of the festival all the locals make small boats of banana leaves. Later, they set burning candles upon and lower boats on water. In the evening, all the beaches of Krabi are illuminated with thousands of lights. In November, the island hosts the Festival of the Andaman Sea. The beginning of this colorful festival coincides with the start of the tourist season. Exciting competitions in beach sports, concerts and entertainment for children, an incredible culinary contests and an abundance of colorful fairs are main attributes of that popular holiday. Krabi is the perfect place for those who want to learn more about Thai culture and enjoy beautiful holiday rituals.

This is also a great destination for those looking forward to the New Year. The matter is that in Krabi, the holiday is celebrated not once but as many as three times a year. Firstly, the European New Year is traditionally celebrated on December 31. Secondly, the Chinese New Year is widely popular (due to the large influx of tourists from China), it falls either in January or February. And thirdly, the Thai New Year takes up the baton in April. The European New Year is accompanied by fireworks and street parties with the participation of European tourists. Before the Chinese New Year, locals clean their houses, then morning processions start, followed by festive fireworks in the evening.

But the most colorful holiday is the Thai New Year known as Songkran. Celebrations traditionally begin on April 13, ending on April 15. Bright parades are held in the morning, temples are important spots at this time, all the actions take place around them. Local people carry statues of Buddha on the cars. At this time, one needs to be careful to avoid wetting documents or phones: The thing is that, according to tradition, locals pour water from buckets and shoot everyone they meet on their way from water guns - and among them are not only passersby but also Buddha statues. So if you want wonderful memories, it is still better to leave papers and electronic devices in the hotel and go for the most pleasant impressions - be sure there will be a lot of them.

On December 5, Krabi traditionally celebrates the birthday of the most revered person in Thailand - namely, Bhumibol Adulyadej, the ninth king from the Chakri dynasty. The festival is called "Father's Day", during its celebration portraits of His Majesty are hung on all the streets of Krabi, the streets are also decorated with yellow flags (traditionally the yellow color is the King's color), locals also try to wear yellow. In Krabi, the holiday is as bright as in the Thai capital, with fireworks, parades and public festivities. On this day, it is also customary to congratulate fathers. Another holiday associated with the royal family is celebrated on August 12, when Queen Sirikit was born. This celebration is traditionally called "Mother's Day" when mothers are congratulated accordingly.

Krabi also celebrates a few holidays related to Buddha. First and foremost, this is Visakha Bucha, the birthday of the spiritual teacher, the celebration falls on May or June (the eighth day of the fourth month of the lunar calendar). Bright parades are held in the city, nobody can become sad - even if one wants. Another festival is traditionally celebrated in February and is called Magha Puja, and is dedicated to how the founder of Buddhism taught his followers. Believers celebrate in temples that become crowded at this time. In August, Sat Duan Sip, the Ancestors' Day, is celebrated - the only day of the year when departed relatives can get into our world. Locals collect gifts for them and carry them to shrines.

Shopping in Krabi

Shopping in Krabi authentic goods, best outlets, malls and boutiques

In the province of Krabi, interesting shops can be found literally at every step. The city of Ao Nang has many shops aimed at fans of chic outfits. For example, the famous fashion shop Andy the Tailor where you can buy a lot of ready-made garments or order tailoring of desired ones. Luxurious dresses will be tailored here for ladies, and men will be offered jackets and trousers in various styles. A large selection of shops where one can pick clothes for every taste is presented all around.

Krabi is also famous for its original markets so you can go to Maharaj Market in search of fresh seafood and local delicacies. This market is one of the largest in the province, it presents a huge range of exotic fruits and vegetables. Here you can also try seafood cooked over an open fire. On the market, you can buy different varieties of homemade cheese and fresh seafood from local farmers. Here they sell a lot of packaged salads and other foods that savvy travelers would like.

A real shopping attraction of Krabi is its night markets. One of the most attractive in this category is the Chao Fah Night Market. This market resembles a kind of open-air restaurant. In addition to fresh products, popular ready-to-eat meals are also sold here. Recreation areas with tables are equipped right in the marketplace. Chao Fah Night is popular not only among tourists but also among locals who often go here for dinner.

In many large cities you can visit modern shopping malls, and among the largest ones is Klong Muang Plaza. Clothing and footwear shops are available to visitors in this shopping center. Here you can buy new beach accessories or take a walk in search of popular souvenirs and local delicacies. Apart from the shops, the mall houses a popular massage parlor so visitors can always relax after long shopping trips.

Pay special attention to local jewelry stores. In Ao Nang, you can visit the large salon Hinmalayan Treasures. All ladies will be pleased with an abundance of exclusive jewelry, chic necklaces and gemstone pendants, and hundreds more types of rings and earrings. In this salon, you can buy luxury jewelry with natural pearls and mother of pearl, which are much cheaper here than in many European countries.

Among all other souvenir shops, it's worth highlighting Paka Krabi located in Krabi Town. Here, beautiful T-shirts with national symbols and pretty handmade bags are available to customers. Women will surely appreciate inexpensive costume jewelry, as well as traditional magnets, trinkets and other small souvenirs offered in this shop.

A must-have for ladies in the capital is Panchivaprai. This store specializes in organic cosmetics, the range of products is really wide. Essential oils, wonderful creams and hair care products, bath salts and organic soaps are just some of the products presented in this store. The cost of produce remains at an affordable level so it's hardly possible to leave the store without buying anything.

The main outlet in the region called Outlet Village is located in Krabi Town. People go to this modern shopping center for cheap clothes, shoes, and accessories, it presents a large selection of products of decent quality. The outlet will appeal to both men and women, as it has a large sports shop, as well as shopping pavilions selling bags, wallets and other accessories.

Go to Riley Beach to explore the famous shopping mall Fashion House, if you're hunting for locally produced textiles. This shopping center is a single complex with a studio where customers can order tailoring of any item they like. Here you can get yourself an exclusive bedding set, a fashionable coat or evening dress - the choice of fabrics presented in the shopping center is huge.

Tips for tourists

Preparing your trip to Krabi: advices & hints things to do and to obey

1. Be sure to take a sunscreen with you. Going to a beach or just walking without a hat is not recommended. Even in cloudy weather it is likely to get the severe sunburn.

2. While walking through the parks and nature reserves it's necessary to listen to the guide. Don't touch unknown plants in any case. Personal belongings should be closely monitored, as nature reserves are inhabited by quite a lot of monkeys. They can deftly snatch the bag or camera, and it will be very difficult to return your stuff.

3. Markets and shops accept only local currency, any other is simply forbidden. It's better to change money in banks that serve visitors from Monday to Friday, from 8:00 - 9:00 am to 4:00 - 5:00 pm.

4. Tourists have to go shopping with plenty of notes with small face value. In no way you have to pay with large denominations on markets and in small private shops, as it is likely to receive the

change with counterfeit notes. If you try to repay them later in a large store or restaurant, then such action would be considered a serious offense.

5. Shops and shopping centers open early, no later than 9:00 am. Major shopping centers are open every day until late at night; a working day in small shops usually ends at 6:00 pm. Local jewelry remains the popular souvenir among tourists; it's better to buy it in specialty stores.

6. Tap water shouldn't be used for drinking and cooking. It is better to purchase bottled water in stores; in restaurants and cafes it isn't recommended to order drinks with ice.

7. Main voltage is 220 V; in almost all hotels necessary electrical adapters and connectors are available on request.

8. The best time to go on vacation is the period from late October to early April. In the rest of the year heavy rainfall is possible, which can disrupt the recreation program.

9. In public places you need to be quiet, and not to raise your voice when speaking in any case, as such behavior is considered a sign of bad manners. Upon entering the restaurant, the shop or the bank you need to greet and to smile - these are rules of the local etiquette.

Best Things to Do in Krabi

Discover the best things to do in Krabi. The whole region is fast becoming a very popular tourist destination and has loads to do. Krabi has its own airport which handles international and domestic flights. Considering the miles and miles of spectacular coastline, lush hinterland and lots of leisure activities at hand, it's no wonder that the area is growing as a tourist hotspot.

Still, one of the main attractions of Krabi is that it still is relatively untouched. The province still manages to retain its natural charm. See below Krabi's best attractions, landmarks and things to do. From picturesque tropical islands to pristine natural parks, there's a lot for you to see in Krabi.

Railay Beach - Krabi

Railay Beach is, in fact, a small peninsula which counts four beaches. Now on every savvy traveller's list, Railay is nevertheless one of Thailand's most sought-after beach areas. Just south of Ao Nang Beach, around a rocky headland and accessible only by boat, Railay presents a tranquil and extraordinary world.

In just one small peninsula you'll find gorgeous white sand beaches, soaring limestone cliffs, viewpoints, caves and a lagoon hidden inside the cliffs, shaped and fed by the changing tides. All within walking distance!

At Railay there are no roads; only footpaths. No buses, no cars, just longtail boats. Although it's actually connected to the mainland, the spectacular Phra Nang Peninsular is effectively cut off from the rest of Krabi by limestone headlands and steep jungle valleys; the only access is by sea. The very picture of tropical paradise, with no roads and no hassle, Railay offers lazy days, adventure forays and chilled-out evenings.

First Time in Railay – What to Do
Commonly called Railay Beach, Railay is in fact a peninsula located a 10-minute's long-tail boat

ride south of the downtown hub of Ao Nang, the prime resort town in Krabi Province. Railay is an intriguing place due to its remoteness, and to the fact it can only be accessed by boat. The land access is technically impossible because of the huge limestone cliffs that effectively cut off this exotic paradise from the rest of the mainland.

Railay Peninsula hosts four beaches a walking distance from each other: Railay Beach West and East, Phra Nang Beach, and Tonsai Beach; the latter can be reached on foot from Railay Beach West only at low tide. Each beach attracts a different type of guest. Most Railay hotels are located in the central part of the headland just a stroll away from the beaches. Tonsai Beach, which is on the western side of the peninsula, has its own accommodation choices.

Railay at a Glance

Railay has all the assets to offer you a memorable holiday off the beaten track. Thanks to its remoteness and to the fact it can only be visited by boat, this small peninsula seems to be stuck a light-year-away from our modern world. A holiday in Railay is almost like travelling back in time. Fortunately, the seclusion of the area doesn't mean that the hotels and the satellite businesses do not feature modern technologies such as Wi-Fi connection and mobile phone communication.

What's Good About Railay:

- ✓ Four beaches to explore
- ✓ Exotic, tropical landscape
- ✓ Wide range of hotel prices
- ✓ Many hotels right on the beach

What Is Less Good:

- ✓ Only accessible by boat
- ✓ Barely developed
- ✓ Few shopping opportunities

Things You Can Do in Railay

Featuring four beaches, Railay is obviously the right place to enjoy nautical activities, especially sea kayaking. The limestone nature of the cliffs that separate Railay from the mainland makes this area the prime rock climbing destination in south Thailand. Last but not least, Railay is also a great port of embarkation to go island hopping. If this is your first time in Railay, the following things to do should be on your bucket-list

Accessible only from the sea, Railay's four beaches Tonsai, Railay West, Railay East and Phra Nang are situated between towering limestone cliffs. Railay West is one of the south of Thailand's most impressive, atmospheric and beautiful beaches and is outstanding any time of day (or night). It's possible to walk between these beaches to compare and contrast their attractions.

Phra Nang is not as developed as the others and has silky-soft sand while Railay East can seem a little rough but is nevertheless the centre of nightlife in the area. Don't believe the (sometimes crooked) boatmen who say that you can't reach Tonsai on foot. You can, through the jungle.

Phra Nang Beach - Krabi

Phra Nang Beach (not to be confused with nearby Ao Nang) is the southern strip of sand in Railay Bay. With 450 metres in length, and reachable in a mere 20-minute long-tail boat trip directly from Ao Nang, or by foot from Railay East (about 10-minute walk) if you are already on the peninsula, it is more popular and busier than Railay West during high season (Nov- April).

With duvet-soft sand, clear shallow water for safe swimming, two small islands (Koh Rang Nok and Nai), coral reef, and caves, Ao Phra Nang has all the ingredients of a perfect beach. All this, set against a backdrop of picturesque limestone cliffs that provide natural shade from the hot afternoon sun, and offer rock climbers one of the most stunning sites for this thrilling activity in Krabi Province.

At the bottom of the limestone cliffs lies the Princess Cave or Tham Phra Nang Nok. Dedicated to an ancient fertility goddess, the cave contains a strange combination of large phallic symbols (lingams), garlands and offerings in the hope of increased potency and prosperity. A bizarre sight for some foreign visitors, local fishermen still leave offerings even though it became a local tourist attraction. A second cave - right next to the original - is also used for offerings and prayers; it contains the same kind of items as the original cave.

Adventurous explorers can also find a cave at the western end of the beach: accessible with the help of ropes, it is not a too challenging hike, and the reward is a fantastic view to the Andaman Sea and the islands lying off the coast.

Phra Nang is a great beach to simply hang out. Just offshore, are the two tiny islands mentioned above, which you can walk to at low tide along a sand bar and go snorkelling. There's only one accommodation option on Phra Nang Beach, the deluxe Rayavadee Resort which unobtrusively occupies part of the beach. At lunch time, long-tail boats customized as floating kitchens beach along the shore to serve a great choice of local and international dishes as well as fresh drinks to hungry beachgoers.

Phra Nang Beach
How to get there: From Ao Nang, get a long-tail boat ticket (100 baht) at the booth located along the beach road (toward its southern end). You also could join a half or full island-hopping day trip by speedboat.

Railay West - Krabi

Railay West is the main beach in Railay. As the main 'port of arrival' on the peninsula, it offers perfect soft sand on a 600-metre-long, rather wide, beach, and a tiny community of friendly locals and expats who run small stores (convenience, beachwear, handicraft), bars and restaurants on Railay Walking Street.

The Walking Street leads to a pathway that goes straight across the peninsula and links Railay West with Railay East skirting past dozens of small bungalows dotted around the area. You can also walk along the beach at Railay East and along the base of the cliffs to Phra Nang Beach (About 15 minutes). Four hotels are also settled directly on Railay West beachfront: Railay Village Resort & Spa, Railay Bay Resort and Spa, Sand Sea Resort, and Rayavadee Resort.

Both Railay West and Phra Nang have surrounding cliffs that twist into fantastic shapes, weathered by the wind and rain over time. Trees and shrubs cling precariously to the rock face, as do rock climbers who come here for sun, sand and the challenge of an overhang or a vertical wall. Most people, however, just come to relax and enjoy.

At sunset, the beach is a hive of activity with boats arriving and departing, impromptu games of football and takraw (sort of volleyball played with the feet) and people taking a stroll. The beach faces west, so its a great place to just sit and watch the stunning tropical sunset framed by limestone cliffs.

Railay West

How to get there: From Ao Nang, get a long-tail boat ticket (100 baht) at the booth located along the beach road (toward its southern end).

Railay East - Krabi

Railay East could not be more different than the three other beaches of Railay: it is a narrow beach and home to mangroves, local fishing boats and many birds. It's also the most convenient place to find a long-tail taxi boat to Krabi Town. A cement footpath has been built all along the beach and even further north, as it carries on two kilometres after The Last Bar – which used to be the previous end of the beach. It is a great addition for jogging or strolling. A new bar & restaurant named Tew Lay has been built on this path.

A few local and hotel restaurants line the beach, providing welcome shade and a drink while you wait for your boat near the floating dock (a jetty made of large plastic boxes). At night they form the focal point of the Railay high season party scene. Bars like Skunk, Joy's and The Last Bar offer an eclectic mix of fire-twirlers, pumping music and care-free vibes until it's time to head back to your bungalow.

Along the pathway which links to Railay West (about a 10-minute walk) are dozens of small bungalows giving the feeling of a small self-contained village, which indeed it is, with restaurants and convenience stores in addition to the many bungalows.

Accommodation can also be found around the north end of Railay East, nearer the nightlife scene. If you're interested in climbing, check out the climbing schools also located at this end of the beach. Diamond Cave is one of the main attractions in Railay East: featuring a wooden walkway and proper lighting, you can get away from the sun for a short visit in this cave housing bats and featuring superb rock formations (entrance fee is 40 baht).

You can also walk from Railay East to Phra Nang Beach (about 10 minutes.) The two beaches are connected by a path which follows the base of the cliffs bordered by caves and stalactites. On this path, you'll also find the challenging track that leads to the mysterious Hidden Railay Lagoon (Sa Phra Nang); similar to the Hongs in Phang Nga Bay, and only worth a visit at high tide, Railay Lagoon is very difficult to access due to the very steep and muddy path.

Tonsai Beach - Krabi

Tonsai Beach is the lesser known beach of Railay peninsula. At a length of around 600 metres, it runs on from Railay West, separated by a rock face at high tide, and faces south. Stuck between two high limestone cliffs, it can be reached by foot from Railay West at low tide. Quieter than the other beaches, Tonsai Beach hosts a few hotels with names like Dream Valley Resort, Tonsai Bay Resort or Mountain View Resort, as well as some beach restaurants and bars, that makes it really the perfect place to get away from it all.

The beach of Tonsai is not renowned to provide vacationers with great swimming or snorkelling: reefs and rocks right in front of the sand make it dangerous; at low tide, it is almost impossible to beach at Tonsai, even for long-tail boats. A legend says that in the eighties, the beach was owned by an Australian citizen who tried to sell it to Club Med; when the Club Med people came, it was low tide and their long-tail boat could not reach the shore. The Australian then decided to dig a channel with dynamite in a way to make the beach accessible whatever the tide level. Unfortunately, after months of efforts, the channel was still not large enough to be usable, so he gave up. This means the rugged and more untouched vibe around Tonsai remains even today.

Regarding the activities available at Tonsai Beach, visitors can enjoy sea-kayaking (a few stores have kayaks for rent) and scuba diving (a few dive shops are available here). But the main activity on offer at Tonsai remains rock climbing: the tall limestone cliffs surrounding the beach offer the perfect playground for experienced rock climbers (the grades of climbing difficulty vary here from 5 to 8c). There is a climbing school on site if you'd like to learn this thrilling activity.

Tonsai Beach
How to get there: From Ao Nang, get a long-tail boat ticket (100 baht) at the booth located along the beach road (toward its southern end). At low tide, you can get there on foot from Railay West.

Koh Poda - Krabi

Koh Poda is one the most popular islands in Krabi archipelago. Located just six kilometres offshore from Ao Nang, it roughly takes 25 minutes to get there by long-tail boat. The price for a return ticket is about 300 baht per person; note that if you travel alone, you will have to wait for the long-tail boat to be full according to its capacity before you set off.

Mu Koh Poda or Poda Island group consists of four islands: Koh Poda, Koh Kai, Koh Tap and Koh Mor. Koh Poda is the largest of the group despite its area being no more than a kilometre in diameter. Covered with palm and pine trees and almost entirely encircled by a soft white sand beach, it is every inch the stunning tropical getaway. A coral reef lies about 20 metres from the beach with a variety of sea life. The irresistible combination of excellent snorkelling, scenery and soft sand make the island a popular choice with snorkelers and sea kayakers, but surprisingly, it's not that crowded.

Koh Poda
Remarks: Koh Poda can be visited all year round. (Not affected by the monsoon - May - October)

How to get there: From Ao Nang, get a long-tail boat ticket at the booth located along the beach road (toward its southern end). You also could join a half or full island-hopping day trip by speedboat.

Krabi Emerald Pool

Krabi Emerald Pool (Sa Morakot) is a unique attraction in southern Thailand. Krabi is well-known for areas of outstanding natural beauty and one place that should make your must-see list is the Emerald Pool in the Thung Teao Forest Natural Park, an unusual lowland forest rich in bio-diversity, complete with a nature trail and a crystal pond.

Located in the Khao Pra-Bang Kram area, the nature trek is a superb place to spot rare animals and plant species including the Pitta Gurney bird which was once considered extinct. The forest is lush with age-old trees stretching up to the sky, unusual forest creatures and limestone foothills that open onto a dazzling emerald pool.

There is a park office close by at Ban Bang Teao which offers some information although their primary goal is to ensure that the no-hunting zone is enforced and that no harm comes to this naturally beautiful sanctuary.

Emerald Pool Highlights

Thung Teao Forest National Park is a virgin rainforest home to spectacular flora and fauna unseen elsewhere in Thailand. A 2.7 kilometres nature trail provides a superb vantage point, plus there's a waterfall to explore, although the major attraction is the emerald pool also known as the crystal pool. The emerald waters are wonderfully warm and crystal clear making them great for swimming in, there's even a small ladder to help you get in and out.

It's a stunning eco-tourist spot with visually beautiful aquamarine colours surrounded by tropical rain forest and a fantastic spot for bird watchers. The journey to the emerald pool begins at the wildlife sanctuary office and takes around 800 metres through a well-trodden forest path or alternatively you can follow the longer nature trail which winds through spectacular tropical rain forest - one of the few remaining in Southern Thailand. The nature trek should be taken slowly so that you get a chance to see some of the very rare animals living in this ancient woodland.

Krabi Emerald Pool
Opening Hours: open every day during daylight hours
Location: Thung Teao Forest Natural Park is situated in the Khao Pra-Bang Khram area which

is located next to the Bang Teao Village, about one hours drive from Ao Nang.

Remarks: Bring mosquito repellent and water if you're planning on taking the nature trail, also do not leave any valuables such as cameras unattended as you swim as thefts have been known.

Price Range: Admission is 100 baht for children and 200 baht for adults

How to get there: head towards Amphur Klong Thom on highway No.4/ Turn left onto highway 4038 then right onto the rural road following the signs towards the Emerald Pool Waterfall.

Koh Hong (Hong Island) in Krabi

Koh Hong is a get away island on the Krabi coastline. Spend your day doing nothing but lazing on virgin sands. This wonderful group of tiny islands offers breathtaking scenery, soft white-sand beaches, coral reefs and a beautiful lagoon. It's where you can enjoy swimming, kayaking, snorkeling, scuba diving, fishing, sunbathing, hiking, and picnicking. Koh Hong is part if Than Bok Khorani National Park and it's only open for day visits with no overnight stays allowed.

Highlights of Koh Hong

The Koh Hong archipelago consists of about a dozen islands but most are so tiny that they don't have beaches of their own but the biggest island has several lovely beaches. However things rarely get crowded here as there's so much to do.

What puts Koh Hong on top of many visitors' itineraries is its spectacular rock formation and its breathtaking natural lagoon surrounding by majestic limestone formations. There is only one way to enter this inner lake; the entrance channel's width is about 10 metres, therefore you can easily get in with a long-tail boat or a kayak. The water is not deep, just about one metre, perfect for leisurely swim.

Good to know about Koh Hong

Tour companies usually include Koh Hong in their Krabi islands trip packages, it's likely that you will get to stop for lunch at Koh Hong as part of the trips and you can expect to spend plenty of time here afterwards.

You can also hire a boat from the Krabi long-tail co-ops for a day trip. They usually include a few different islands such as Koh Hong and Koh Lading. The cost is less than 3,000 baht for round trip and they can take up to six people.

Koh Hong
Opening Hours: Best time to go is November to April
Location: About five miles from the mainland Krabi Province.
Tel: TAT Krabi Tel: +66(0) 75-622163 or +66(0) 75-612811-2 or Than Bok Khorani National Park ,
Koh Hong Ranger Station Tel: +66 (0) 75 681096

Price Range: Admission Fee: 400 baht (adults) and 200 baht (children)
How to get there: You can hire a speedboat from Nopparathara Beach, Krabi. The trip will last only about 15 minutes. If you are going by a long-tail boat, it will take up to 40 minutes to get there.

Krabi Tiger Cave

Krabi Tiger Cave offers a genuine spiritual experience in stunning natural surroundings. Tiger Cave Temple or Wat Tham Sua sits 5 km northeast from Krabi Town centre. It is one of

Thailand's finest natural wonders, and it's definitely worth a visit. The temple here is a warren of natural limestone caves formed inside at the foot of an impressive cliff. There are beautiful icons in the main temple cave, but the real attraction here is the 'footprint of the Buddha'.

To get to this historic site you need to hike 1,237 steps up the limestone tower. Krabi Tiger Cave offers you a challenging climb, especially in the Thai climate. Those who make it to the top are compensated with panoramic 360 degree views. The panorama encompasses the Andaman Sea, dramatic limestone cliff formations, and verdant rainforests. You'll also discover 'the Buddha's footprint' that lies on the terrace. The vistas are particularly stunning at sunrise and sunset. It's also the best time to climb up and avoid the heat.

Krabi Tiger Cave Highlights

Arriving at Krabi Tiger Cave, spend some time exploring the lower levels before taking the challenging climb up. Legend has it that a tiger once made the main cave his home. This gave the temple its name, Wat (temple) Tham (cave) Sua (tiger). There are still tiger footprints on the floor of the lower temple. You might want to purchase some bananas by the entrance to feed the many monkey occupants. Just remember that they can bite and scratch so don't get too close.

Thereafter take one of the two staircases up to the top. The one which is located close to the Chinese fertility goddess statue is slightly easier. Either way the climb is strenuous and should not be taken lightly. The steps are uneven and steep jutting up the mountain. You should allow up to one hour to make the climb, enjoying the rest stops and vantage points on the way up.

Krabi Tiger Cave
Remarks: Dress respectfully and remember to take a bottle of water and some snacks with you before to climb. Also, remove any jewellery, sunglasses or valuable items which may be taken by the playful monkeys. A visit is best scheduled early in the morning or late afternoon to avoid the midday sun.

How to get there: Krabi Tiger Cave Temple is located about three kilometres from Krabi town and easiest reached by mini-bus, taxi or tuk-tuk. You should arrange a fare with the tuk-tuk driver in advance. Another option is to take a traditional Thai public bus also known as a songthaew from either Krabi town or from Ao Nang. The public bus makes for a really cheap and interesting option where you'll see plenty of Thai sights and sounds along the way. The bus stops at the road next to Wat Tham Sua and from there it takes about 20 minutes on foot.

Ko Phi Phi

The Phi Phi islands are an archipelago of 6 islands, with the 2 main islands being Phi Phi Don and Phi Phi Leh. Just a 45-minute speedboat trip or a 90-minute ferryboat ride from either Phuket or Krabi, these picture postcard islands are excellent tropical getaways in Southeast Asia.

Phi Phi has pristine beaches, stunning rock formations, and vivid turquoise waters teeming with colourful marine life. The larger and inhabited Phi Phi Don attracts hundreds of travellers to its lovely shores, while the smaller uninhabited Phi Phi Leh has beautiful bays and beaches, including the iconic Maya Bay.

There's quite a selection of things to do in Phi Phi, even on the archipelago's tiniest islands. The larger of the Phi Phi islands are ringed by beautiful beaches and private bays. Above the azure seas, you have striking limestone cliffs, white sands and nodding palms. Below, there's colourful coral reefs and vibrant sea life.

There are very few manmade attractions on Phi Phi. It's mostly all about the natural beauty of this amazing part of Thailand. Check out our comprehensive guide to what to do in Phi Phi below, and don't forget to pack your camera for your trip!

Best Things to Do in Phi Phi Islands

Discover the best things to do in Phi Phi Islands, otherwise known as Koh Phi Phi in Thailand. Located 43 km west from the coast of Krabi, this small archipelago consists of 6 islands: Koh Phi Phi Don, Koh Phi Phi Leh, Koh Bida Nok, Koh Bida Nai, Koh Phai (Bamboo Island), and Koh Young (Mosquito Island). The only inhabited island – and the largest – of the group is Koh Phi Phi Don.

Our list of top things to see and do in Phi Phi below features the most popular sites the island have to offer. The natural beauty of the area is second to none and provides a great choice of tours and activities – you're easily spoilt for choice on things to do in Phi Phi.

Koh Phi Phi Leh & Maya Bay
Koh Phi Phi Leh is the second-largest island in the Phi Phi archipelago. The uninhabited island

(apart from rangers stationed in Hat Nopharat Thara-Mu Koh Phi Phi National Park) has only 1 beach that's located in Maya Bay.

With clear-crystal waters, white sand, and lush tropical vegetation, Maya Bay gathers all the postcard clichés in one place. During high season (November to April), its international fame attracts visitors from around the world. Another cool spot on the northeastern side of Koh Phi Phi Leh is the Viking Cave, which has rock paintings of what look like Viking ship

Phi Phi Viewpoint

Phi Phi Viewpoint is one of the highpoints (in more ways than one) of a visit to Phi Phi Don. The viewpoint is set at an elevation of around 186 metres, which isn't really that high. If you're feeling energetic, it's a brisk 20-minute walk up or a leisurely 30-minute stroll to the top.

The journey up isn't that difficult at all as the path is well-trodden and paved most of the way. There's plenty of places to rest if need be. Starting from the Reggae Bar, head towards Loh Dalum Bay and you'll see signs for the viewpoint. Don't forget to buy water at the bottom!

Highlights of Phi Phi Viewpoint
When you arrive at the top, you'll be pleased to find cold drinks, ice creams and other snacks on sale. The hammocks will be extremely welcome for some and the flat rocks make comfortable seats. The view is, of course, magnificent. You can see Phi Phi Leh and all of both Tonsai Village and Loh Dalum bays. From here, you'll be able to appreciate the 'dumbbell' shape of the island and marvel at the island's beauty.

The best time to come from a photography point of view is before 10am as the sun will be behind you which brings out the colour of the sea. If there's a light shower while you're at the top you might be lucky enough to see a rainbow over Tonsai Village.

For those who want to go further, 3 paths lead to bays on the other side. The middle path takes you to Rantee Beach, about a 20-minute walk, and the paths to the left and right lead to Pak Nam Beach and Ao Toh Koh respectively, both some 45 minutes away.

These are not nature trails as such; just tracks used by locals to save on the cost of a longtail to and from Ton Sai. There are some tricky bits, but nothing that requires a mountaineering diploma.

Bamboo Island in Phi Phi Archipelago

Bamboo Island ('Koh Phai' in Thai) is one of the 6 islands belonging to the Phi Phi archipelago in the southern Thai province of Krabi. Approximately 5 km northeast of Koh Phi Phi Don, it's a tropical dream come true. The island measures around 600 metres wide by 700 metres long, and is entirely surrounded by a strip of white sand.

Bamboo Island hosts great snorkelling opportunities with the presence of superb coral reefs lying at a short distance off its shore, mostly on its western side. A small bar serves drinks and snacks. Day and overnight trips (sleeping in tents) are available from Koh Phi Phi Don, or you could visit the island on a Phi Phi day trip by speedboat from Phuket

Bamboo Island – or Koh Pai – is the most north-easterly island of the Phi Phi archipelago. Lying approximately 5 km off the northern tip of Koh Phi Phi Don, this island is a stunning tropical hot spot that offers the perfect getaway from crowds. While a few tours from Phuket make a stop on this island after lunch, it's usually never too crowded.

Measuring roughly 600 metres wide by 700 metres long, the island is shaped almost like a heart, and is surrounded by a strip of white sand. Its central part is covered with lush vegetation, including casuarina and bamboo trees. On the north-eastern side of the island, under the shade of the trees, a small bar serves drinks and snacks.

Highlights of Bamboo Island

Bamboo Island offers great snorkelling opportunities. Between Phi Phi Don and Bamboo

Island stands a notable coral reef known as Hin Klang, which provides visitors with the sensation of swimming in an aquarium. Closer to the beach, the island is almost entirely surrounded by a reef that spreads up to 500 metres from the shore.

You can hire a long-tail boat in Tonsai Village or Sea Gypsies Village on Laem Thong Beach to get to Bamboo Island. The journey will take around 40 minutes from Tonsai and 15 minutes from Laem Thong Beach. Day and overnight trips (sleeping in tents) are available from Koh Phi Phi Don, or you could visit the island on a Phi Phi day trip by speedboat from Krabi or Phuket. Since Bamboo Island belongs to a national park, you'll have to pay an entrance fee to get there.

Bamboo Island in Phi Phi Archipelago

Location: Bamboo Island, Ao Nang, Krabi 81000, Thailand

Viking Cave in Phi Phi Island

Viking Cave is one of the most notable sites on Koh Phi Phi Leh, located at the bottom of a tall limestone cliff on the north-eastern side of the island. It takes roughly 30 minutes to get there by long-tail boat from Tonsai Bay (the main pier in Phi Phi Islands).

Known as Tham Phaya Nak in Thai, Viking Cave owes its name to the paintings found on the eastern southern walls of the cave: they represent various types of boats, including what resembles a Scandinavian Drakkar or Viking ship. These paintings were possibly done by sailors taking shelter in the cave during a storm

Highlights of Viking Cave

Visiting Viking Cave is an excellent way to discover one of the most profitable local industries – the harvesting of swiftlet birds' nests. Particularly prized in Chinese culture, these edible nests are believed to promote good health, specifically for the skin. A local legend says that a long time ago, sailors lost their boat during a storm and got stuck without food on one of the limestone islands lying in the mouth of the Phang Nga Bay.

A cave located on this island was home to a colony of swiftlets, and the men were able to survive by eating their nests. The harvest of bird's nests is rather a risky job – scaffolds are built with bamboo, on which the hunters climb in the dark to collect these valuable nests.

Diving in Phi Phi

Diving is one of the prime activities in Phi Phi. The island counts a large number of serious and professional PADI dive centres dispensing courses – from *Discover Scuba Diving* to *Divemaster* – and day trips to the many world-class dive sites available in and around Phi Phi's waters.

Amongst the most notable dive sites of the area, Shark Point, Anemone Reef and the King Cruiser Wreck are located to the west between Phi Phi Islands and Phuket. Maya Bay, Koh Bida Nok and Nai are located on and near Koh Phi Phi Leh – all of these sites can be reached in less than 40 minutes from Koh Phi Phi Don.

Shark watching tours

Shark watching is a popular activity for nature-loving visitors to Phi Phi Island. The most popular spot for this tour is off the eastern end of Long Beach, a few hundred metres from the shore. It's known as Phi Phi Small Shark Point (there's another Shark Point off the west coast of Phi Phi Don Island, which is only accessible by scuba diving). This unique encounter allows you to swim with one of the ocean's most misunderstood creatures and such tours are usually fascinating and dramatic experiences.

All shark tours include safety precautions and proper equipment. Blacktip reef sharks are the most common species in the shallow waters around Koh Phi Phi, measuring around 1 metre in length.

Shark-watching tours on Koh Phi Phi Don are one of the most popular things to do on the island. The waters around Phi Phi Islands host a good number of placid black-tip and leopard sharks. Phi Phi's shark watching tours usually start very early – about 6am – and last half a day. Led by a professional guide, these tours are done in small groups with full snorkelling equipment provided.

The most renowned site for shark watching is the small 'shark point' located 800 metres off Long Beach (there's another Shark Point off Phi Phi Don's west coast, which can only be visited on diving tours. Exciting and educational, a shark-watching tour will leave you with unforgettable memories. One of the most experienced shark tour companies is The Adventure Club.

Highlights of shark watching tours in Phi Phi

Some people might feel scared as they dip their feet into the water, which is a perfectly natural reaction. However, as you overcome your fear and try to calm yourself, you'll notice that these blacktip sharks aren't agressive or harmful. Rather, they're quite timid.

If you show signs of fear, they might actually swim away. You might get to encounter a couple of sharks surrounding the place, swimming in circles.

The activity is typically done in the morning, depending on the flow of the tides. Each tour only accepts a small group per batch as to not disrupt and scare the sharks.

One of the most experienced shark-watching tour companies in Koh Phi Phi is The Adventure Club. Shark watching tours are definitely an opportunity you should not miss when you're on Phi Phi Island.

Location: Central Tonsai Village, Ko Phi Phi Don, Ao Nang, Krabi, Thailand
Open: Daily from 8am to 10pm
Phone: +66 (0)81 895 1334

Moo Dee Bay

Moo Dee Bay ('Loh Moo Dee' in Thai) has a 500-metre-long white sand beach that offers pleasant snorkelling opportunities, mostly at both ends. Situated on the east coast of Koh Phi Phi Don, it's an excellent escape from the crowd.

A Rastafarian shack sells food and drinks here. The easiest way to get to Moo Dee Bay by hiring a long-tail boat near Tonsai Pier, which will take you to the beach in about 20 minutes – you can put your bargaining skills to the test when asking for the fee, with around 200 baht being the norm.

Highlights of Moo Dee Bay in Phi Phi

Moo Dee Beach is really a cool spot that's very quiet and relaxing in the morning. It's often visited by those on day trips from Phuket and Krabi, which can perturb its peacefulness in the afternoon until about 3.30pm. The beach offers pleasant snorkelling opportunities, mostly at both ends of the bay.

A beach shack sells food and drinks – note prices can be very steep, so it's best to bring your own bottle and snacks.

Rock Climbing in Phi Phi

If you're interested in rock climbing during your holiday, Krabi Province (including Koh Phi Phi) is one of the best places for rock climbing in southern Thailand. Thanks to towering natural limestone cliffs that make up most of its topography, you'll find world-class sites such as Tonsai Beach and Diamond Cave in Railay all along the coast.

Phi Phi Don Island lies around 42 km off the coast of Krabi, sharing the same topography. You can find thrilling climbing walls both on Koh Phi Phi Don and Koh Phi Phi Leh. Many local shops offer information on routes that are properly rebolted with stainless steel or titanium bolts. Professional companies often organise half- and full-day climbing tours led by highly trained instructors.

Rock climbing walls in Phi Phi Islands

We've compiled a list of the most notable rock climbing walls in the Phi Phi Islands, many of which were first discovered and bolted by French climbers – which is why many routes are named in French.

Tonsai Tower is at the western end of Tonsai Bay on Koh Phi Phi Don. Spanning 200 metres in height, the limestone formation has 48 bolted routes catering to all levels of difficulty, from beginners to advanced.

Drinking Wall is on the way to Tonsai West, right behind a large, empty field where locals play football late most afternoons. It offers a dozen challenging bolted routes (grades 5 to 7c) in a lush environment. Visit before 11am if you want to get some sunlight while climbing. Note: beware of snakes in the rainy season.

Ao Ling Wall (Monkey Bay Wall) lies just south of Tonsai Tower. It's quite challenging to get there on foot, so it's best to hire a long-tail boat. It offers a good choice of routes (12) graded between 3 and 8b. Popular routes include *Ligne de Vie* (Lifeline), *La Main de Buddha* (Hand of Buddha), and *Trip Master Monkey.*

Hin Tak is just south of Ao Ling Wall and overlooks Tonsai Bay. It has at least 19 routes graded from 5 to 8b. Its location makes it only accessible by boat. The most popular route here is *Happy Banana* – it's graded 6a with 1 move to 6b+.

Hua Ling Wall (Monkey Head Wall) is at the northern tip of Nui Beach on the west coast of Koh Phi Phi Don. You have to hire a long-tail boat at Loh Dalum to get there, but access is tricky at low tide. It has 4 routes graded from 6a+ to 6c.

Ao Pilay Wall is on the west coast of Koh Phi Phi Leh. It roughly takes 20 minutes to get there by long-tail boat from Tonsai Bay in Koh Phi Phi Don. This tricky wall counts 7 routes graded from 6a to 7b. The most spectacular route is *Four Beers of Singha*, a 6a+ route that goes up to 35 metres.

Maya Bay has 2 rock climbing walls – the first is at the northern end of the beach itself, offering 5 routes between 7 (*Le Lotus Bleu*) and 18 metres (*Travelling Shoes*) in height, which are graded from 5+ to 7a+. The second wall is inland, on the beach's northern end. There are a couple of 10-metre-high routes, called the *Culture of Pleasure* (7b grade) and *Japanese Girl* (6a+ grade).

Captain Bob's Booze Cruise

Captain Bob's Booze Cruise is one of the most unique excursions around Phi Phi Islands. This trip involves hopping on a boat and touring the perimeter of the island while boozing it up and enjoying a party atmosphere. It takes you cruising on a 9-metre sailboat towards Maya Bay, Monkey Beach, and Loh Sama Bay.

During the tour, you will also get a chance to witness the magnificent sunset from Wang Long Cove. Onboard, you can also play your own music by plugging in your smartphone into the boat's built-in sound system. Other activities on the tour include cliff jumping, island hopping, fishing, snorkelling, and exploring Viking Cave.

Highlights of Captain Bob's Booze Cruise

Captain Bob's Booze Cruise usually departs in small groups from Tonsai Bay, about 100 metres from the pier. The tour starts at 1pm and ends at 7pm every day. If you're lucky, Captain Bob himself might even join your tour, which will certainly make for a memorable experience.

The tour is reasonably priced and inclusive of lunch, fruit, snacks, and unlimited beer. You can also upgrade your tour to include a diving activity. For a more intimate experience, private day trips can be arranged for groups of up to 10 people.

Captain Bob's Booze Cruise
Location: Phi Phi Cabana Bookings Office,
12/37 Moo 1 Chalong, Muang, Phuket 83130,
Thailand
Open: Daily from 10am to 8pm
Phone: +66 (0)89 678 0898

Shipwrecked Boat Tour in Phi Phi

The Shipwrecked Boat Tour is a fun cruise that combines exotic seascapes with a party atmosphere. You will sail to fascinating spots in the Andaman Sea off the coast of Phi Phi Island while enjoying a wide range of cocktails. The yacht hosts a fun party, making it very popular with younger travellers, but everyone is welcome to join the fun.

Shipwrecked Boat Tour stops at 7 famous destinations around the Phi Phi Islands. Explore the famous Maya Bay, Monkey Beach, Viking Cave, Table Coral City Reefs, Pi Leh Lagoon, and Snake Cave, as well as a secret location to watch the sunset from.

Highlights of Shipwrecked Boat Tour in Phi Phi

An excursion with the Shipwrecked Boat Tour includes a freshly prepared lunch, dinner, and snacks. Snorkelling gear is also available for you to use.

You can enjoy free unlimited alcohol onboard, including beers and cocktails. Juices, water, and sodas are also available. The trip starts from 11am until 9pm. The crew will warmly welcome and provide you with free T-shirts, meals, shots, party games, and a photo opportunity.

Shipwrecked Boat Tour in Phi Phi
Location: 108 Moo 7, Shipwrecked Bar Phi Phi, Koh Phi Phi, Ao Nang, Krabi 81000, Thailand
Phone: +66 (0)81 818 8333

Koh Tup and Koh Mor in Krabi

Koh Tap (also spelled Koh Tup, Koh Tub or Koh Thap) and Koh Mor are two tiny islands that belong to the Mu Koh Poda group. Located approximately nine kilometres from Ao Nang, it takes about 30 minutes to reach them by long-tail boat from the prime resort towns in Krabi Province. These two islets are linked by a sandbar which, at low tide, also enables you to walk to Koh Kai (Chicken Island), situated some 500m away.

The popularity of Koh Tap and Koh Mor is due to their specific shape, as both sides of the sand bar offer great snorkelling in crystal clear waters. This sandbar is called 'talay waek' in Thai, which means 'divided sea'. A short hike to Koh Tap's summit offers a cool viewpoint to the other islands around.

The best way to get to these islands is to join the Krabi Four-Island tour by speedboat (or any similar excursion). Alternatively, if you just want to go there to spend the day, you could pack a lunch, and simply take a long-tail boat from Ao Nang, Railay, Klong Muang or Nopparat Thara. It will cost you about 300 baht per person to get there from Ao Nang. Note that you will have to wait for the boat to have at least eight passengers before setting off.

Krabi Hot Springs (Klong Thom)

Therapeutic and soothing, the Krabi Hot Springs are 'hot tubs' crafted into smooth rock channelling water from deep rooted thermal springs located in volcanic chambers. The waters average 35-40 degree Celsius and are brimming with natural mineral salts which are claimed to cure all manner of health complaints including rheumatism and sciatica. The sensation is utterly relaxing and the environment is certainly unique, imagine sitting in a bath tub hollowed out from nature's stone and surrounded by rainforest. These jungle baths feed into a cool stream which is perfect for dipping and diving into.

Located about 70 kilometres from Krabi town, the hot springs are in the heart of a small jungle preserve and close to the Khao Phra Bang Khram Nature Reserve. Situated in the same reserve as the Emerald Pool and Thung Teao Forest Natural Park, it's worth taking the time to combine all of these wonderful eco-spots in one nature filled day.

Krabi Hot Springs Highlights
Idyllically located under tropical rainforest canopies, the cascading waters of the hot springs offer a unique way of getting right back to nature and leaving the world behind with a rare treat of pure mineral salts in their natural environment. The Jacuzzi type baths are perfect for sharing and can be filled right to the top with warm running water supplied fresh from the thermal springs. The hot springs are unusual in that they

cascade forming a waterfall that pours into a stream below.

When you've finished taking a hydrotherapy bath, there are plenty of places to soak up the surroundings including a trip to the crystal or emerald pool or by following a nature trek all located within the same park. The hot springs are easy to find located via a winding boardwalk, to get to the cool stream that the warm waters cascade into, follow the winding path down for a refreshing dip.

Krabi Hot Springs
Opening Hours: from 07:00 - 18:00
Remarks: You will need to bring a beach towel, sandals and of course swimwear.
Price Range: Entrance is charged at 90 baht for the springs or you can pay 200 baht and also access the Khao Phra Bang Khram Nature Reserve and Crystal/Emerald Pool.

How to get there: To get to Klong Thom Hot Springs you can choose to book a tour, or hire a taxi to take you there direct. Car rental is also an option with the drive taking around 40 minutes. Follow highway no 4 towards Amphur Klong Thom turning onto highway 4038; thereafter follow Sukhanphiban 2 road and the signs for 12 kilometres to the hot springs and the Emerald Pool.

Ao Luk Attractions, Krabi

Ao Luk mangrove and caves is a suitable field for exploration and soft-adventure experiences in Krabi Province. Ao Luk District is located approximately 40km north of Krabi Town on the road to Phang Nga Town and enjoys an outstandingly preserved natural environment. This area is rural and hosts two parks: Than Bok

Khorani and Khao Phanom Bencha National Parks.

Tall limestone cliffs similar to those found in Phang Nga Bay dot the hilly lush landscape, and along the coast, mangrove forest and limestone cliffs offer sea kayakers an exciting tropical playground. The small town of Ao Luk is a genuine southern Thailand village that has been cut in two by the Krabi-Phang Nga highway. It is a charming place to have a short rest for people driving from Phuket to Krabi Town as a few street food stalls and a 7-Eleven allow tired drivers to grab a snack and a drink.

Than Bok Khorani National Park
In Ao Luk on the main road to Phang Nga-Krabi, turn left (when coming from Krabi Town) at the traffic light in the direction of Laem Sak. Bok Khorani National Park Headquarters is located on

the left about two kilometres after the traffic light. The National Park headquarters offers a trail through the rainforest and limestone hills with waterfalls, caves and even a small Buddhist temple.

Popular with locals as it offers a cool, shady forest and a number of small pools, it is an ideal location for picnics and a swim and it gets busy at weekends. Bring your own snacks or sample barbecued chicken, fruit and snacks from local vendors at the entrance of the park.

Opening Hours: 06.00 - 18.00 daily

Ao Luk Mangrove & Caves
Along the Ao Luk-Laem Sak Road, turn right approximately 3.5km after Than Bok Khorani National Park Headquarters and continue for 1.5km then turn left to reach a large parking

space on the side of Tha Pring Canal. Here you can hire a long-tail boat for a few hundred baht and discover three caves in the mangroves: Tham Phi Hua To, Tham Lod Neua, and Tham Lod Tai. The latter is a long narrow limestone tunnel with stalactites and stalagmites and is best visited by long-tail boat at low tide.

Tham Phi Hua Toh/Hua Galok is a large cave which used to be a burial site some 3,000 years ago. Some paintings on the ceiling of the cave are dated from this time. Tham Phi Hua Tho means 'Big-headed Ghost Cave', due to the fact that the cave, viewed from Tha Pring Canal, looks like a huge limestone face. Apart from the paintings, the cave also displays some strangely shaped rocks: a dragon's head and a crocodile head. There are other caves located in this area: Tham Prah Cave, the site of the Khao Prah Suhn

Yah Tah Rahm Meditation Centre, Tham Pet Cave, named because the walls of the cave reflect light like a diamond.

Health and Safety

There is an increased concern about terrorism risk in the whole of Southeast Asia, including Thailand. Caution is advised, particularly in places and venues frequented by tourists and on public transportation.

Because of political unrest, travel to several southern provinces, including Narathiwat, Pattani, Yala, and Songkhla, is currently advised against. Arson, bombings, and killings have taken place irradically since January of 2004. Travelers to rural or remote areas should be accompanied by a guide, who can prevent accidental border crossings

On a less life-threatening scale (for the most part), travelers to Krabi, should exercise caution when approached by anyone attempting to sell gems, or to refer you to gem dealers. Over a thousand reports a year are made by visitors scammed by fraudulent gem dealers. Credit card fraud is also on the increase.

Though violent attacks on tourists are rare, pickpocketing and purse-snatching, especially in crowded, touristy areas, is not. Tourists have been known to have had unattended food and/or drinks drugged for the purpose of robbery while on trains or in bars. Finally, as unsavory as it is to mention, the prostitution industry is alive and thriving in Thailand, and women are not held in high regard. Though foreign women traveling in Krabi are relatively safe, it's still wise to take precautions: dress conservatively and avoid night travel alone.

Krabi Town Weather and When to Go

Best time to visit is November to May; you'll find glorious sunshine all day. Yet, because Krabi is sheltered by mountains it is still very cool and breezy especially at night.

August and September tend to be rainy months but generally all the rest of the year is pretty nice and warm.

And the water is warm too (28*C) so great to jump into the water and try snorkelling or diving.

Its worth noting that due to the amount of limestone karsts jutting up out of the land and sea causing cloud lift, one area can be bathed in hot sunshine, while just round the corner, there can be a downpour.

January: Hot days, Cool nights, small chance of rain. A great month to visit Krabi.

February: Hot days, Warm nights, small chance of rain

March: Hot days, cooling slightly at night, small chance of rain

April: Very Hot days, cooling slightly at night, small chance of rain (historically the hottest and driest month of the year)

May: Hot days, late afternoon showers (normally only last a matter of minutes)

June: Hot days, late afternoon showers (normally only last a matter of minutes)

July: Hot days, late afternoon or evening showers, high waves possible

August: Fair chance of showers in the daytime between sunshine, high waves possible

September: Wettest month of the year, high waves likely

October: Weather improving, mainly sunny, afternoon showers possible

November: Hot & sunny mainly, still a risk of showers

December: One of the best times to visit – hot & sunny with little chance of rain. Nice & cool at night.

Transportation

Arriving and Departing

Krabi Airport is small and compact, and about 20 minutes drive from Krabi Town. Make sure to bring adequate cash in Thai baht for transportation. Taxis charge a fixed price of 600 baht for a car to Ao Nang that supposedly only has room for three people. You can get a van with more capacity for 1000 baht. It may be worthwhile to share a vehicle with some fellow passengers from your flight.

Airport buses run to Krabi Town (90 Baht per person) and Ao Nang Beach (150 Baht per person). You will see the airport bus desk as you exit Arrivals. The buses wait in the parking lot and do not depart until they're full or there are no more arriving passengers left.

You can pre-book a Private Car, Luxury SUV, Standard Minibus or Family Minibus (a bit larger). The driver will be holding your name on a board as you exit arrivals. Prices are slightly cheaper than taking an airport taxi on arrival. Example: Aonang - 600 Baht for a private car or 750 Baht for a Minibus

Krabi airport pick-up service: offers private transfers starting at 580-1200 baht.

For those on a tight budget, walk out of the airport terminal building, cross the parking lot and then the main road and flag down the next "songthaew" (local transportation - a converted pick-up truck) heading to Talad Khao Bus Station and/or Krabi Town. From there, you can take another songthaew to the beaches (Ao Nang 50 Baht, Klong Muang 70 Baht).

Bangkok Airport-Transfer: offers private transfers starting at 800 baht.

Krabi Airport Transfers : offers online reservations for private transfers in their luxury Airport Limousines (Toyota Camry) and family vans (Toyota Commuter). Transfers to and from most beaches near Krabi town can be booked without any type of deposit (pay on arrival). Krabi Airport Transfers are operated by a locally owned business with decades of experience.

Krabi Transfers :offers krabi taxi services from airport to your destinations. Travelling around by taxi with driver is possible as per your request.

Best airport and infrastructure

The airport itself boasts of two storeys of well-designed passageways that allowed human traffic to flow smoothly from getting off the plane to immigration to baggage collection. As as one emerges from the glassed corridors of the airport, they are met by throngs of taxi drivers and shuttle bus providers. Having said that, culturally the locals in Krabi are less "pushy" than what has been experienced in many other parts of Thailand. The people are friendly and relaxed, respecful to tourists and clearly proud of their new international airport. Checking into the airport at the end of a holiday was also a pleasant experience - the counters were well-lit, broad and spacious. Right after checking in, one could quickly move through immigration to the large waiting areas. Much to the surprise of many tourists, everything works like clockwork at Krabi International Airport - big kudos to the airport authorities and local provincial managers.

Word on the ground is that Krabi Province is fast becoming the tourist destination that it deservedly should be. As Krabi increases in prominence, nearby Phuket is deemed often by tourists as over-crowded and over-developed and starting to lose its relaxing get-away mood. It is rumoured that Phuket International Airport, which surprises many as the structure and surroundings is a far cry from anyone's expectations of being an international airport, will be demolished for several years of redevelopment to make way for a new airport. Thus, leaving nearby down-south Krabi as the new destination for many international flights.

The Krabi provincial authorities have definitely learnt from the mistakes of other parts of Thailand, and as they started on the land planning and infrastructure building of the province to convert a sleepy little township into a tourist must-go, they have clearly and evidently taken into consideration the need for well paved sidewalks, broad streets leading into the tourist areas, and well light and sign-posted roads leading away from the airport.

And in Ao Nang, the famed tourist strip of Krabi right by the beachfront, shops maintain their lively seaside charm and quaintness. People are friendly and everything seems to take 2 paces slower than most other parts of Thailand. What is most enchanting about Krabi, is how the crowd seems to be different from nearby Phuket - there is a much more gentler family-oriented trend in the tourists who choose Krabi as their holiday destination. For those of us who have discovered the charm and beauty of Krabi, we hope it stays that way for a long time to come before commercialism taints its unique serenity away

Getting Around

Krabi, Thailand, is a port town, affording the visitor several options for getting around. Open-air buses, converted trucks, motorcycle "taxis," and river taxis operate regular services to accomodate the traveler. Fares are reasonable and faces are often smiling.

These river taxis are long-tail boats, often tended by sea gypsies, who will "ship" you any of the myriad of islands around Krabi. Many of the long-tail boats are colorful, bright and inviting. Pay a little more and the operator will serve as your tour guide as well.

Motorcycle taxi drivers congregate at public functions and tourist areas such as markets. Though the fare may be inexpensive, the ride may not be worth the risk. Drivers are fast, and accicents on these motorcycle taxis are common throughout Thailand. Enough said, hopefully. Of course, there are also regular, vehicular taxis, the drivers of which will serve as guides for an added fee. The open-air buses and converted trucks run regularly and stop just about anywhere. Flag one down with the wave of your hand.

Traffic conditions in Thailand can be realistically classified as unsafe. Recklessness and consumption of drugs and alcohol cause numerous accidents. Congestion is common, as is failure by the majority to adhere to traffic rules. Roads are paved and there are four-lane roads between many cities.

Perhaps it is needless to say, after all this, that walking can be risky anywhere, including Krabi. It is highly recommended that pedestrians use extreme caution when crossing streets, and use overhead walkways whenever possible.

Things to Do in Krabi Town

Day Trips

Krabi is a haven for scuba diving and snorkeling. There are several local sites offering good, adventurous caves and caverns, plus some fabulous dive locations: Shark Point, Anemone Reef (as the names say it all, great for leopard shark watching, covered with anemone in bright plethora of colors), and Phi Phi. You can take diving course and get a PADI certification while you're there.

Rock Climbing and Trekking

Take a day trekking tour to Emerald Pool. Definitely a trip on the land side is worth it; don't expect the wildest rainforest, but actually there is many places that come close. Emerald pool and Hotsprings are the most popular ones and also with most people. To avoid the crowd a little try to pay a few 100 of baht(2-4 euro) more and then make it a private tour. Then you can go new unexplored places or atleast not have to be depending on a whole bus of others.

<u>Sea Kayaking</u>

The huge mangroves and prehistoric limestone Karsts that are the hallmark of Krabi's outstanding geography, create a labyrinth of sea canals dotted with caves in an extremely rich eco-system that is only possible to explore by Kayak.

Many companies now offer guided tours to the stunning Phra Nang bay, especially at Boh Tor in the north of Krabi near Ao Luk, which is the main are for mangrove kayaking tours. Here you can paddle through sea caves with incredible stalactite and stalagmite formations, and also walk through a huge cave with many stone age cave paintings. There are even child-friendly companies that conduct 2-day courses.

Events & Festivals

Help Krabi and all of Thailand sing "Happy Birthday" to her majesty, Queen Sirikit of Thailand in August. All over the country, monuments and historical landmarks are decorated with colored lights and ornaments. Music and dance is big in Thai culture, and the International Festival of Dance, held annually in Bangkok every September, reflects this.

Performances by artists the world over give the festival a truly international flavor.

For a good laugh (and watch your step), attend the Elephant Polo Tournament in Hua Hin in late September. Teams from around the world compete, and other elephant-associated activities take place, like the Elephant Parade. Hopefully no Elephant Face-painting, though.

October marks the Setting Adrift of the Chao Le Boats from Kho Lanta Island, an annual rite performed by Krabi's Sea Gypsies, in hopes of gaining prosperity and good fortune in the coming year. Nearby Phuket honors Thailand's king every December with its King's Cup Regatta. Begun in 1987, the Regatta has grown to be the biggest boat race in all of Asia. A personal envoy of the king presents the winner's cup to the victor in the culminating ceremony.

Opening the Andaman Sea is a yearly event that takes place in November. This festival marks the official beginning of the tourist season in Krabi, with parades, musical performances, races, and open-air markets featuring locally-produced goods.

Hike to Huai To Waterfall (half day)

The park is about 30 minute drive from Ao Nang Beach or Krabi town. You will pay about 100 baht ($3) per person for entry. The area is very pretty with giant trees near the parking area. They have a small shops with food there and nice grounds. There are two routes to the waterfall one easy and one more challenging and steep. If you take the long route there and back it is a bit strenuous. The hike is about 35 minutes if you're in shape. Recommended this for younger and stronger hikers. Also wear something more than flip flops.

The waterfall has an upper (20 ft) and lower (50 ft) section. The upper has a nice pool for swimming. It might be a good to take the long way up and shorter route down. This way you can see both sections and have a restful return. Half day for the entire trip including driving would be more than enough time.

Museums & Attractions

Krabi has four national parks to enjoy. The Khao Sok is a rainforest habitat with a large variety of birds and animals, and is a popular for day trippers and campers. Than Bokkhorani features natural springs, limestone cliffs, and a lot of (real) monkey play. Pa Tung Tieo is south of Krabi and is a lowland rainforest. The last national park's name is probably longer than the park is wide: Hat Nopharat Thara-Mu Ko Phi Phi. Forget trying to say it, just visit the beaches and beauty it encompasses. Many parts of this park are only accessible by boat, so hire a guide and sail away.

The waters of Krabi's coastline offer some excellent oppotunities for deep diving or shallow snorkeling among coral reefs. Deep sea fishing may turn up sailfish, tuna, mackerel, or mahi mahi. Tour the areas many islands (some of them deserted) on a guided tour, or rent a sea kayak and head out on your own adventure. Rock climbing on Krabi's limestone cliffs draws climbers from all over.

The Wat Khlong Thom Museum, on Phetchakasem Highway, displays artifacts excavated from a bead mound: stone tools, stone and clay animals, bronze tools, and beads. With all the limestone on the island, there's got to be fossils, right? Right. Found within the confines of Hat Nopharat National Park, is Fossil Cemetery and nearby Fossil Museum, displays fossils and telling the history of the area.

Off the Beaten Path

You'll find lots of off-the-beaten-track places in Krabi and vicinity, and almost as many Buddha idols hanging around nearby, like Big Brother. One interesting place to visit that's north of town is the Tiger's Paw, a rock formation that derives its name from its similarity to the paw of a tiger. Climb the 1,237 steps to see a view of Krabi and some great scenery as well as a giant Buddha looking along with you.

If you're a diver, there are lots and lots of places to go for a day of underwater ballet in and around Krabi. For experienced divers, there's Shark Point, which features the wreck of a cruiser where you'll likely see Leopard Sharks, Reef Sharks, and Nurse Sharks, as well as Barracuda and Jacks. Or take a boat tour of Krabi's surrounding islands, and stop off to do some snorkeling or shopping.

Hot Springs, to the south of Krabi, is in the middle of a forest, where you can sigh and sink slowly into 35 degree celsius water, and let all your troubles melt away.

Avoid the many alligator farms and animal exhibits unless you enjoy seeing and having your photo taken with a drugged, beleagured animal. Unfortunately, there is a lot of that around.

Scuba Diving

Scuba Diving & Snorkeling Tours
Scuba diving in Krabi is a must do activity, with many dive centers offering everything from one day dive experiences for the complete novice, up to professional level diver courses.

If you've never tried diving before, you can choose from a range of simple introductory dive courses and experience stress free scuba with friendly and professional dive instructors and if you're with the family, any non divers can experience one of the worlds most unique and beautiful seascapes by joining you on your dive and snorkeling excursion.

If you're already a certified diver, knowledgeable PADI Divemasters are ready to guide you on day trips and liveaboards in the fascinating underwater world of the Andaman Sea, one of the most beautiful destinations for snorkeling and diving in South East Asia.

Highlights include the local dive sites at small islands in Ao nang bay or Phi Phi Marine national park, 3 dive "Superdays" at the King Cruiser wreck, Shark Point Marine Sanctuary and Anemone Reef, cavern diving at the amazing grottos at Ko Ha Yai, and even speedboat trips to Hin Daeng and Hin Muang to dive with Mantas and Whale Sharks.

Dive Sites In Krabi..
Ko Ha Yai Caverns and Lagoon -
The Ko Ha Yai Islands are a group of stunning and remote islands situated about a one and a half

hour speedboat trip from the Krabi mainland. The dive sites here are exceptional with (nearly) always amazing visibility, fantastic swim throughs, plus the between dives snorkeling is truly outstanding.

Depths range from 3 to 34 metres with an abundance of marine life attracted by the Islands labyrinth of small caves, caverns and crevices. The first dive includes a cavern with two entrances at 5 and 16 metre depths, with a cathedral like interior that stretches 30 metres above the surface. Light filtering in through the water creates a magical atmosphere and since the surface is accessible at any time during the dive even less experienced diver can visit this truly unforgetable site.

Dive Level - Novice - Intermediate - Experienced - Advanced

Hin Daeng (Red Rock)

Without doubt one of Thailands best dive sites, Hin daeng is located far to the south of Krabi hi Phi Islands it's long distance from shore means it is only available by speedboat or liveaboard. Divers are drawn to its remote location by the almost constant presence of Whale Sharks and Manta Rays, as well as large schools of other pelagic fish and reef sharks.

The Southern side of the pinnacle drops off almost straight down to a depth of over 60 meters making it the deepest wall dive in Thailand. This unusual rock although teeming with smaller sea life, a sparse coating of soft corals and a few sea fans seems almost barren when compared with the rest of the site, but is a good place to hang out for Whale Sharks and Manta sightings.

The Eastern side gently slopes off along two long narrow ridges until they disappear into unreachable depths. By descending along the wall to a depth of 30 meters you are likely to encounter huge schools of Trevallies, Jacks and Tuna sometimes so thick they appear as a solid wall of silver. Large Barracudas sweep past the ridge as they stalk the feeding Needle-Fish and Long Toms. The sheer amount of marine life you find here makes the long journey worth every minute.

Dive Level - Experienced - Advanced
Hin Muang (Purple Rock)
This site is totally submerged and is located just a few hundred meters north of Hin Daeng. The site gains it's name from it's covereing of lush purple soft corals and anemones, compared with the relatively barren rocks of Hin Daeng it's as if you

are swimming in an entirely different ocean and not just a short distance away.

The limestone pinnacle stretches more than 200 meters in length and in some places is less than 20 meters in width. The almost vertical walls are carpeted with anemones and colorful sea fans and the numerous little caves, ledges, and rocky outcroppings provide shelter for virtually every underwater creature found in Southeast Asia, and the rich eco system seems to be a magnet for every Manta Ray in the region, with Mantas regularly in groups of 5 or more hanging out here for days.

Dive Level - Experienced - Advanced
Phi Phi Islands Marine National Park
South of Ao Nang are the twin islands of Phi Phi Ley and Phi Phi Don with stunning sites suitable for every level of diver and snorkeler - shallow

sheltered bays, soft coral walls and deep reef dives. Living in and around the colorful array of coral gardens, stag horn coral fields and huge sea fans you will find a every type of sea life – masses of schooling fish, turtles grazing on beautiful anemones and on the sandy bottom reclusive leopard sharks can be found resting.

Some of the best sites are "the Bidas" – Bida Nok, Bida Nai and Hin Bida, three sites teeming with life and just a short 45 minutes cruise by speedboat. For novice divers and snorkelers the Phi Phi area is an ideal destination, with superb shallow water coral bays and beaches.

Dive Level - Beginner - Novice - Intermediate - Experienced - Advanced
Local Islands
The closest sites to the Krabi mainland are at the stunning limestone islands in Ao Nang bay. The

islands are surrounded by shallow water, fringing coral reefs where diving depths reach 20 meters and visibility is around 8 -10 meters.

A huge variety of juvenile reef fish inhabit the shallow waters found here before moving off to the more dangerous deeper waters further offshore. regular visitors are all types of clownfish, yellowfin barracuda, titan triggerfish and black tip reef sharks. Some of the nicest sites include Ko See, Ko Ha, Ko Taloo, Ko Daeng, Ko Mae Urai and Ko Yawa Sam.

In early 2013 two new dive sites were added to the area with the sinking of two ex Royal Thai Navy LCT's (Landing Craft Tank), close to the Island iof Koh Yawa Sam, at a depth of 22m. These sites are suited for experienced or advnced level divers only, but should prove to be excellent sites as they are colonised by marine life and develop rapidly into artificial coral reefs.

Dive Level - Beginner - Novice - Intermediate - Experienced - Advanced
When To Dive in Krabi..
Although diving is a year round activity in Krabi, the main dive season runs from October to May, with conditions improving steadily through October to December. The best conditions are arguablly January to April, but if you're not a fair weather diver, the low season months can offer some excellent and very uncrowded diving

Shell Cemetery / Gastropod Fossil

This is located a few Kms outside of Ao Nang and a Tuk Tuk there and back will cost about B400..

According to Lonely Planet Thailand Guide (2009), entrance fee is B50pp however it is B200pp (B100 for children).

The appraoch down some steps has the usual souvenir vendors, There are a few fossil beaches in the area, all very similar in nature. The main area itself, located at the entrance point, is basically a very small beach which looks as though its covered in broken concrete slabs, which on closer examination are in fact the gastropod fossils embedded in a fossilised layer.

There isnt actually a huge amount to see or do and for money, unless you are a major fossil fan, there are almost certainly better ways to spend your time and money.

Ko Phi Phi Quick Travel Guide for New Travelers

Understand

<u>The named islands are:</u>

- ✓ Ko Phi Phi Don, the largest and only populated island. You will not believe the amount of development this place has undergone, which is almost entirely restricted to the narrow sandbar separating two of the island's most prominent beaches. Marketed as a tropical island, the flurry of activity around the numerous supermarkets, restaurants, tattoo parlors and ATMs may just surprise you.

- ✓ Ko Phi Phi Leh, a smaller island to the south, popularised when parts of the movie "The Beach" were filmed there. Uninhabited apart from bird nest harvesters and a few

Maya Bay wardens; expect plenty of tourists during daylight hours, especially in Maya Bay, also known as 'the beach'. Setting foot here requires a 500 baht entrance fee, which may or may not be included in your tour price. As of 2018, Maya Bay has been closed to tourists indefinitely in efforts to perserve the ecosystems and coral reefs.

- ✓ Ko Mai Phai ('Bamboo Island'), a small low-lying islet to the north of Phi Phi Don with a beach and some very limited snorkeling.

- ✓ Ko Yung ('Mosquito Island') is north of Ko Phi Phi Don. The island has a stone beach in the east and small sandy beaches at the foot of the hills. Patches of rather unhealthy coral may be found off the shore, surrounded a shocking number of sea urchins.

- ✓ Bida Nok and Bida Nai, two small adjacent limestone karsts to the south of Phi Phi Leh, with near-vertical cliff walls rising from the sea.

Most of the development of Phi Phi Don is situated in or around Ton Sai village, which is on the low, sandy isthmus that joins the two hilly spurs that comprise the rest of the island. There are also other, quieter resorts on Long Beach, Laem Thong, and at other less accessible areas of the island.

Ko Phi Phi was devastated by the Indian Ocean tsunami of December 2004, when nearly all of the island's infrastructure was wiped out. Redevelopment has, however, been swift, and services are back with building regulations in place to limit the height of new buildings to preserve the island's stunning views.

Climate

Weather in the region is tropical - there are only two seasons: the hot season from late January to April, and the rainy season from May to December. Temperatures during the year average 25ºC to 32ºC (77ºF to 89.6ºF) and the yearly rainfall averages 2569 mm. Unlike in say, Europe, the rain in this region comes down heavily over short periods.

History

From archaeological discoveries, it is believed that the area was one of the oldest communities in Thailand dating back to the prehistoric period. It is believed that this province may have taken its name after the meaning of Krabi, which means sword. This may have stemmed from a legend that an ancient sword was unearthed prior to the city's founding.

The name Phi Phi (pronounced 'pee pee') originates from Malay, the original name for the islands was "Pulao Pi ah Pi". The name refers to the mangrove wood found there.

Geography

Ko Phi Phi is considered to be one of the most naturally beautiful islands in the world (in fact, there are six islands in Phi Phi). They lie 50 km southeast of Phuket and are part of Had Nopparattara-Ko Phi Phi National Park which is home to an abundance of corals and amazing marine life. There are limestone mountains with cliffs, caves and long white sandy beaches. The national park covers a total area of 242,437 rai.

Phi Phi Don and Phi Phi Leh are the largest and most well-known islands.

There are two villages on Ko Phi Phi under the administration of the Ao Nang Sub-district, Muang District, Krabi Province.

Ko Phi Phi comprises 6 islands, 2 of them main – Phi Phi Don and Phi Phi Le. The islands are surrounded by the Andaman Sea.

Culture
Krabi is a melting pot of Buddhists, Thai-Chinese, Muslims and even sea gypsies. The majority of the population in the rural areas is Muslim. Krabi however, does not suffer from any religious tension and the folk live in peace and harmony. Outside of the provincial town, the rural folk speak with a thick southern dialect which is difficult for even other Thais to understand.

With this kind of mixture, Krabi is always celebrating something be it part of Thai

Buddhist, Thai-Chinese, or Thai-Islamic tradition. Visitors can also enjoy the annual boat-launching ceremonies of the sea gypsies and various longtail boat races.

Art
The art of batik is practiced by the locals. There are also a lot of Krabi handicrafts, such as pineapple paper.

Tourism
Tourism on Ko Phi Phi, like the rest of Krabi province, has exploded only very recently. In the early 1990s only the most adventurous travelers visited the island, staying in only the most basic accommodation costing the likes of 50-100 baht a night. Nowadays, however, the place has turned into one of the major destinations for visitors to Thailand. The development however,

is still nothing on a par with the likes of Phuket or Ko Samui.

However, presently, budget backpackers can still get a cheap room away from the beach, up the hill a bit.

Ko Phi Phi has plenty of night life, but if that isn't your cup of tea, then there are lots of really quiet places to chill out and take it easy.

Get in
By boat
Tonsai Pier, situated in the center of Tonsai Bay, north of of Phi Phi Don. It's the island's main pier and the busiest. You can purchase tickets online as well. Their prices are pretty much the same as what you will get directly at the pier. Definitely cheaper than most tour agencies as there is no commission involved. Phuket Harbour Holiday

To/From Phuket: Ferries leave from Phuket daily at 08:30, 11:00, 13:30 and 15:00 via Rassada Pier or Sea Angel Pier. 1.5-2 hrs. 250-800 baht. Possible to get 300-350 baht one-way tickets as part of a deal with a guest house stay. Official price at Rassada pier is 600 for one way or 1000 for return, so buy in advance or be prepared for some negotiating. Note that one-way tickets from Phi Phi to Phuket are 300-350 baht at Tonsai Pier or 200-250 from quest houses at island. You can get from the Phuket Airport to Rassada Pier by meter taxi for around 500 baht. It's about a 30 km drive and takes 45 minutes depending on traffic and weather.

From Ao Nang: Ferry leave from Ao Nang once daily at 09:30 via Nopparat Thara Pier. 2 hrs.

From Rai Leh: -Ferry leaves from Rai Leh once daily at 09:45 via Railay Bay. 1.45 hrs. There's no actual pier, you will transfer by longtail boats to ferry. Same ferry from Ao Nang.

From Krabi Town: Ferries leave from Krabi Town daily at 09:00, 10:30, 13:30, 15:00 and 16:00 via Klong Jilad Pier. 1.3-1.45 hrs. 300-500 baht. 400 baht in December 2014 from PP Family, office right by the pier in town, incl. songthaew to the pier outside town. The normal passenger ferry does not leave from the centre of town anymore, but from a new passenger port (Klong Jilard Pier Tel. 0 7562 0052) about 3 km outside Krabi Town. Free taxi transfer to the pier should be included in the price of your ticket. Many times they'll take you to a travel agent near the Chao Fah Pier and sell you additional accommodations or services. Only ever buy the ticket you need. They add additional ferries during peak season.

From Ko Lanta: Ferries leave from Ko Lanta daily at 08:00 and 13:00 via Saladan Pier. 1 hrs. 200-350 baht as of January 2015.

There is a 20 baht per person fee required on the pier for "keeping Ko Phi Phi clean". Unfortunately, there is still plenty of rubbish on the beaches. Tickets can be purchased on-line or on the dock, from tourist offices, most local guest houses and hotels. Prices vary depending on how far into town you walk before buying. Also, not all ferries are of equal quality.

- ✓ Andaman Wave Master is the only company that will take you for free to the north of Phi Phi after the stop at TonSai Pier. In April 2007, a ferry operated by Andaman Wave

Master caught fire and sank, and all aboard were forced to jump into the sea. Fortunately, nearby vessels were quickly able to rescue all the passengers, and no casualties occurred.

✓ The Sea Angel ferries are quite nice with big flat screen TVs and refreshments. These are sold on-line as first-class ferries.

✓ The ferries run by Chao Koh group, particularly the smallest "Pichamon IV" are often overcrowded and appear to be very poorly maintained, which does not inspire confidence, however they are launching a new mega boat beginning of 2010.

✓ The ferries run by PP Family are larger and seem more suited to the task.

✓ The ferries run by Phi Phi Cruiser take just over two hours and do not depart on time until packed to the brim, but they include complimentary cookies and instant coffee (if taking the morning crossing). For an additional fee, you can purchase a "VIP ticket" which also includes snorkeling and a buffet lunch on Phi Phi Don.

Other tour vessels visit the island from several Phuket-based resorts, usually on day trips, the price for a speedboat from Rawai Beach was quoted at 15,000 baht return(or one way) for up to 6 people (Dec 6 2007). There are many speedboats operating directly from the beach but it may be best to book the day before as most seem to be on away on trips during the day. Speedboats can also be chartered from other nearby locations, but at a very high price.

By all-inclusive tour

Small Agencies selling all-inclusive day trips from Phuket are all over Patong town, and most everywhere else on Phuket Island. Circa late January 2011 - booked a lengthier "half day" hour tour via speedboat negotiated to 1,400 baht/person (from the pamphlet printed price of 3,000 baht). The tour included 6 different stops, a free buffet lunch on Phi Phi Don, snorkel usage, and minibus transport to and from the Patong Beach hotel. This set-up seems incredibly common, and one should be able to find similar deals sold anywhere on Phuket that tourists frequent. Don't buy a trip from the back seat of a a taxi from the Airport...

Things to keep in mind:

- ✓ The lower end priced speedboat tours (what most people book, including the above description) take approximately 25- 30 passengers per 2-engine speedboat and 30- 45 passengers on 3-engine speedboats.

- ✓ The higher end tours take up to 18 passengers on 2-engine speedboats.

- ✓ Tour desks will tell you anything to get your money. It would be best to contact the actual company directly to check prices/services, though 99.9%+ of tourists go through agencies so...don't feel too bad for negotiating the typical way. Remember safety wear a life jacket, don't travel on speedboats if you are pregnant, or have back pains or recurring spinal injury.

By plane
Krabi International Airport (KBV) is about 10 km from the city limits, 15 km from the city centre, 40 km from Ao Nang and 23 km from Had Yao.

Thai Airways operates daily direct flights to/from Bangkok, likewise Air Asia from Bangkok and Kuala Lumpur. Bangkok Airways flies direct to/from Krabi and Ko Samui nearly every day of the week and to/from. Nok Air operates daily flights to Krabi from Bangkok (Don Muang).

For more information, contact:

- ✓ Thai Airways International Public Company Limited: Tel. 1566, 0 2280 0060, 0 2628 2000, 0 2356 1111, 0 7570 1591 – 93 or visit .

- ✓ Krabi International Airport, Tel. 0 7563 6541-2

- ✓ Air Asia Airlines: Tel. 0 2515 9999 or visit .

- ✓ Nok Air: Tel. 0 2627 2000 or 1318 or visit . It offers daily flight+ferry services from Bangkok to Phi Phi v.v. by flying with Nok Air from Bangkok to Krabi and transferred on a ferry to Phi Phi. This can be booked directly from their website.

- ✓ Bangkok Airways 0 2655 5555, 0 2265 5678 .

The international departure tax surcharge is 700 baht but is included in most tickets now; domestic departure tax is included in the price of the flight.

National Car Rental and Budget Car Rental have a branch at the airport; motorcycle taxi rides are available outside the terminal.

Krabi Limousine (tel. +66-75692073) has a desk inside the terminal and provides "limousine taxi" (using large air-conditioned sedans) transport to Krabi for 500 baht; Phuket for 2500 baht. Krabi.com offers taxi and minibus (mini-vans) for less however travellers have to make deposit payment of 200 baht on-line via credit card.

An air-conditioned Airport Bus service started in 2007, fares are 90 baht to Krabi. The bus service meets all incoming flights and serves most outgoing flights (note: it is not possible to catch the first 1-2-go plane in the morning with the new airport bus service) A songthaew to Krabi town is 40 baht from the road outside. Going to the airport they will drop you right at the departure terminal.

By bus
Buses from Bangkok's Southern Bus Terminal (tel. +66 2 4351199) to Krabi take about 12 hours and depart as follows:

- ✓ VIP bus - 07:20 - 1,055 baht

- ✓ Note, there is also a VIP overnight bus from Bangkok leaving in the evening. Prices are 1,300-1,400 when booked via an agency.
- ✓ First class bus - 19:00 - 680 baht
- ✓ Second class bus - 07:30, 19:00, 19:30, 21:00 - 378 baht

Shuttle buses run between Krabi airport and Phuket airport several times a day. There are also regular buses that make the 2 hour run. There are buses to Krabi from every provincial town in the south.

By car
From Bangkok:

1. Proceed along Hwy 4, passing Phetchaburi–Prachuap Khiri Khan–Chumphon–Ranong–Phang Nga, to Krabi. The total distance is 946 km.

1. Travel along Hwy 4 onto Hwy 41 at Chumphon via Amphoe Lang Suan and Amphoe Chaiya, Surat Thani. Proceed towards Amphoe Wiang Sa, change to Hwy 4035 for Amphoe Ao Luek, and switch back to Hwy 4 again to Krabi. This route is 814 km.

From Phuket:

Proceed along Hwy 402 and Hwy 4. The total distance is 176 km.

By train
The nearest train station to Krabi is in Trang province which is just south of Krabi.

Get around

Phi Phi officially has no motorised transport, though there are a few motorcycles with truck side-cars, usually used for goods and construction material transport. Transport on land is by foot or bicycle, but in the populated areas of Ton Sai, nowhere is more than about ten minutes' walk from anywhere else. Long-tail taxi-boats ply between all beaches; on Phi Phi Don, you can also walk to any beach. From Ton Sai to Long Beach, expect to pay 100 baht/person in the afternoon, at least 150 baht at night. To have a complete boat to yourself, expect to pay at least 200 baht.

Wheelbarrows are used to transport goods, including your luggage if you like. Expect free "transport" from the pier to your room, but not necessarily in the opposite direction.

The most common ways to get around on Ko Phi Phi are by foot and by long-tail boat. As with most everything in an area like this, the price for long-tail boats is a negotiation. Hint: Take some foam earplugs for the long-tail boat rides... it's a fun ride but the engines are loud and after 45 minutes it can get to you. The negotiation for longtail boats is usually done according to where you want to go and how many hours you want the trip to last. As an example, 1200 baht for a 6-hour outing to Ko Phi Phi Le and Tonsai Bay from the Holiday Inn Resort.

It's also possible to hike through the island - but if you do so. make sure you take the trail that goes through 3 viewpoints (it's easy to find) - entrance to the first 2 viewpoints is 30 baht and onwards travel to the third viewpoint will cost you another 50 baht, but it's well worth it (views are very nice) and the trail is good - otherwise smaller trails are very overgrown and hard to climb. And have enough water with you - there's little wind in the forest, and there's a lot of heat.

See
Phi Phi Don

This island is the largest of the 6 Phi Phi islands and consists of two main sections. It is on Ton Sai where the original inhabitants settled and is now the home of the main accommodation area. Phi Phi Don is quite stunning and has earned the title of one of the most fantastic islands in the world. Nowadays though, with development, the beaches have paid the price and so they're not quite as spectacular as they were in the days of yesteryear. The landscape however, can never be ruined.

- ✓ Viewpoint - walk up to the Viewpoint (admission 30 baht for the first 2 view points and an additional 50 baht to access the third viewpoint), 186 m above sea level (a very steep walk of between 10-25 minutes, depending on fitness), to get a breathtaking view of the entire island - particularly at dawn or sunset (bring a torch/flashlight). There is a solitary shop at the top of viewpoint #2 selling chilled drinks (no beer) and basic food items. Do not bring any alcohol with you, as the private land is owed by a muslim family that will not allow alcohol consumption on their land. You will be surprised at how narrow the sand strip is between the two main parts of the island. There are a lot of large boulders here, and you can stretch out on one and soak in the view for some time. If health or lack of time prevents you from reaching the viewpoint, you can check out a view almost as spectacular from Banana Bar, Phi Phi's only rooftop bar. The great thing is, you can enjoy a tropical cocktail while you drink up the view!

- ✓ Monkey Beach - accessible on foot or by renting a canoe, or be lazy and charter a longtail boat. Be careful as the monkeys can sometimes be aggressive. Some tourists reports bite attacks and local hospital's number one note is about vaccination against monkey rabies. (Note: you should not feed wildlife.)

- ✓ Fireshow - there are several highly skilled and entertaining fireshows held nightly in several venues on the island, including at Carlito's, Apache Bar, Hippies, Carpe Diem, and The Tia and Millie Sunflower Bar on Lohdalum.

Krabi Travel Destination, Thailand

- ✓ Tsunami Memorial Garden - by the Tia and Millie Sunflower Bar; a beautiful place for quiet contemplation and paying one's respects to the victims of the recent tragedy.

- ✓ Yao Beach Yao Beach, just south of Ton Sai, offers visitors some fantastic views, scenery and coral reefs for snorkelling and scuba diving. This small place is packed out however, with places to stay and so some people do complain that the vicinity has been rather over developed. You can get there either by walking from Ton Sai or taking a long-tail boat.

- ✓ Lanti Beach Next door to Yao Beach, Lanti Beach is very similar in many regards with its great scenery and coral reefs. You can get there on foot.

- ✓ Hin Khao Beach This beach is extremely quiet and can only be reached on foot.

- ✓ Ton Sai Bay (Note this is not the same as Ton Sai near Ao Nang!) Ao Ton Sai is where most of the action is; be it restaurants, bars, hotels or guest houses. Most tourists stay at Ton Sai Bay because of the convenience. Even though it isn't the most beautiful place on Phi Phi, it is still impressive.

- ✓ Laem Tong Laem Thong, located at the very north of the island offers visitors a lovely quiet beach with exhilarating scenery. Accommodation on Laem Thong is aimed at higher spending tourists.

Phi Phi Leh

The second largest of the Phi Phi Islands is extremely beautiful, and pristine, but is uninhabited because it is a national park.

Phaya Naak Cave Cave with prehistoric paintings and edible-nest swiftlets that can be partially visited.

Maya Bay Maya Bay has arguably Phi Phi's most fantastic beach and was the location for the movie The Beach (Leonardo DiCaprio) in 1998. The bay no longer has any coral (dead coral is in abudance), and very few (minnow-sized) fish. There is also a jump spot (~20 m) in one of the creeks behind the beach, and some climbing is possible on the cliff just next to it. You can take a longtail boat to Maya Beach for about 1,500 baht for the whole boat for half a day. It is recommended you arrive at Maya Bay before 08:00, when the place can still be enjoyed in solitude. From 09:00 on, hoards of speedboats with tourists on package tours arrive from Phuket. Another thing to think about when coming to Maya Bay is the time of year. During the high season (Oct-May) you will feel like you are at Disneyland, but during the off season it could be slightly better. Note: Park Rangers have begun enforcement of a National Park entry fee of 100 baht/person. The park police will only attempt to charge you for the "park entrance fee" if you turn up on a longtail boat. The mid-afternoon trip (15:00) is better: you get to catch the sunset as you leave Maya Beach (you can't see the sunset on the beach).

✓ Lohsamah Bay Another bay situated on the west coast of the island, and has a U shape form with a large rock in the middle. There is a very small beach and small caves at the end of a very narrow gorge. There is also a hole in the rock accessible from the water only that leads in the gorge behind Maya Bay beach. It is a very short stroll to go from Lohsama Bay to Maya Bay this way, but be careful depending on the tide and waves, since going through the hole can be a bit challenging depending on the level of fitness and could lead to injuries on the rocks below the surface. If you go this way, you will get completely wet (even at low tide) and therefore will need a waterproof bag in order to bring any non-waterproof electronics.

Other islands
- ✓ Yung Island (Mosquito Island) This island just north of Phi Phi Don has a rocky beach, a bit of coral, and lots of sea urchins.

Depending on where you are dropped off by your boat, there may be a mild current pulling you out to sea. Since tours in Thailand are more or less "every man for himself" novice swimmers may wish to bring safety equipment (such as a lifejacket) or else avoid this spot entirely.

- ✓ Pai Island (Bamboo Island) Not far from Yung Island is Pai Island. On the northern and eastern sides of the island are sandy beaches. There is a swimming/snorkeling area marked off by buoys, but there is very little to see in the water except for bleached coral and the occasional fish. While speedboats drop you directly on the beach, longtails may drop you a few hundred meters further down the shore, after which you will have to hike through a trail lined with garbage, fallen trees, and sand.

Do
Other Activities
- ✓ Shared boat tours - You can join many group tours of islands around Phi Phi Don like Leh, Mosquito island, Bamboo island. You can get cheap THB 300 half - day tour to Phi phi leh with plankton watching from Dorm room operators. Also full day tour Mosquito , Bamboo , Maya Bay etc starting 9:30am to 7pm can be bought for THB 600 from dorm accomodation. This is cheapest you can get.

- ✓ Boat Tours - With the Koh Phi Phi Islands containing six other islands away from the main island of Koh Phi Phi Don there are many beaches to visit such as the Monkey Beach, Maya Bay and Bamboo Island Beach. Also multiple Lagoons and tucked away snorkelling spots. Some boat tours operate with a ferry so you can stay dry while sightseeing the islands. (e.g., or)

✓ Snorkelling - there are two rocks within swimming distance of Long Beach known as "Shark Point" where harmless blacktip reef sharks can be seen. Coral, small giant clams, anemones, and loads of sea urchins can also be spotted. Snorkel trips off Bamboo and Mosquito Island are also sold by many tour groups, but don't expect to see much compared to Long Beach.

✓ Yoga Classes - There are excellent yoga classes on offer daily. Keira of Keiritas Yoga offers classes on Carlito Bars roof-top and in Banyan Villa Gym for people of all levels and experience.

✓ Rock Climbing - there are opportunities for rock climbing on Ko Phi Phi, and a few climbing shops (e.g., or) to rent equipment, find a guide, or take lessons. While not as famous as Rai Leh beach (near Ao Nang), nor with as many routes, the climbing is on similar limestone cliffs, and similarly beautiful. The climbing here also tends to be less crowded than at Rai Leh (near Ao Nang). There are about four walls that are used with some frequency. A half day of climbing (3-4 climbs) is 1,000 baht/person, 1-day (2,000 baht) to 3-day (5,500 baht). Courses are also available for various skill levels. All Climbing Tour / Gear Rental Shops appear to have closed down as of June 2016. If this information is wrong, or new gear rental shops open please remove this note.

- ✓ Kayaking Phi Phi with its dramatic scenery is an ideal location for kayaking. You can either go it alone or with an organized package. Kayaks can be hired either per hour or per day. The typical rate varies between 200 and 300 THB per hour for a two-man kayak. Rent one just before sunset and paddle out some distance into the bay. Even though you cannot see the actual sunset (the direction of the bay and high cliffs on all sides), the colour changes in the sky, coupled with the gentle rocking of the shimmering water is a delight to experience.

- ✓ Cliff Jumping Cliff jumping is fairly new to Ton Sai Bay. There are cliffs from 6 to 16 m that are ideal for cliff jumping due to the depth of water below. Organized tours can be found at Ton Sai. Please note that this is potentially dangerous and can cause injury to people including ear ruptures, and muscle/back injuries. Having said that, as long as you take it easy (not attempt weird flips on your first jump) and follow a simple feet-first technique, it is fairly safe and provides a surge of adrenaline that can only be topped by another, higher leap into the emerald water!

Spa
- ✓ Spa at Zevola Resort & Spa
- ✓ Spa at Phi Phi Island Village, Beach Resort & Spa
- ✓ Spa at PP Princess Diving & Spa Resort
- ✓ Bird Watching The best time of the year for bird watching has to be from Jan to Apr.

Many rare birds are to be seen there: gurneys, finfoots, bigwinged brown kingfishers, egrets, bitterns, herons and more.

✓ Sailing & Cruising Krabi has plenty of anchorages, usually deserted and all so beautiful. There are many charter sailing boats available and some even offer "join-in" day trips for two or more people. Phi Phi offers a variety of ways for sailing and cruising. Longtails can be hired for sunset tours and island excursions, they can be found on any beach. The Original P.P. Sunset Tour is a big boat with plenty of space for snorkelling and viewing the sunsets. Get information about them at The White.

✓ Boat Parties Phi Phi Island is famous for its booze cruises and boat parties (e.g., or) boat parties on Phi Phi Island incorporate sigh-seeing, snorkeling, and other activities with open-bars, live DJ's and party games. Phi Phi Island Boat Parties will often visit many touristic sights such as the Monkey Beach, Maya Bay, Pilleh Lagoon & the Viking Cave.

For a great adventure...visit DragonHeart. Daily sunset and snorkel tours. Tour Phi Phi Leh and cruise into the sunset. Climbing, slacklining, weddings and more! Find them at The Deaf Gecko on Nice Beach. See or email .

✓ Fishing Wannabe fishers can catch the likes of marlin, sailfish barracuda, and tuna.

- ✓ Camping Camping in Maya Bay is possible. See or email . As of October 2014 the department of National Parks ruled the Koh Phi Phi Leh would be closed to tourism after sundown, there is no possibility of camping at Maya Bay. As of June 2018, the DNP set further restrictions, closing Maya Bay indefinitely to tourism

Other Activities

- ✓ Shared boat tours - You can join many group tours of islands around Phi Phi Don like Leh, Mosquito island, Bamboo island. You can get cheap THB 300 half - day tour to Phi phi leh with plankton watching from Dorm room operators. Also full day tour Mosquito , Bamboo , Maya Bay etc starting 9:30am to 7pm can be bought for THB 600 from dorm accomodation. This is cheapest you can get.

- ✓ Boat Tours - With the Koh Phi Phi Islands containing six other islands away from the main island of Koh Phi Phi Don there are many beaches to visit such as the Monkey Beach, Maya Bay and Bamboo Island Beach. Also multiple Lagoons and tucked away snorkeling spots. Some boat tours operate with a ferry so you can stay dry while sightseeing the islands.

- ✓ Snorkelling - there are two rocks within swimming distance of Long Beach known as "Shark Point" where harmless blacktip reef sharks can be seen. Coral, small giant clams, anemones, and loads of sea urchins can also be spotted. Snorkel trips off Bamboo and Mosquito Island are also sold by many tour groups, but don't expect to see much compared to Long Beach.

- ✓ Yoga Classes - There are excellent yoga classes on offer daily. Keira of Keiritas Yoga offers classes on Carlito Bars roof-top and in Banyan Villa Gym for people of all levels and experience.

- ✓ Rock Climbing - there are opportunities for rock climbing on Ko Phi Phi, and a few climbing shops (e.g.,   or   ) to rent equipment, find a guide, or take lessons. While not as famous as Rai Leh beach (near Ao Nang), nor with as many routes, the climbing is on similar limestone cliffs, and similarly beautiful. The climbing here also tends to be less crowded than at Rai Leh (near Ao Nang). There are about four walls that are used with some frequency. A half day of climbing (3-4 climbs) is 1,000 baht/person, 1-day (2,000 baht) to 3-day

(5,500 baht). Courses are also available for various skill levels. All Climbing Tour / Gear Rental Shops appear to have closed down as of June 2016. If this information is wrong, or new gear rental shops open please remove this note.

✓ Kayaking Phi Phi with its dramatic scenery is an ideal location for kayaking. You can either go it alone or with an organized package. Kayaks can be hired either per hour or per day. The typical rate varies between 200 and 300 THB per hour for a two-man kayak. Rent one just before sunset and paddle out some distance into the bay. Even though you cannot see the actual sunset (the direction of the bay and high cliffs on all sides), the colour changes in the sky, coupled with the gentle rocking of the shimmering water is a delight to experience.

✓ Cliff Jumping Cliff jumping is fairly new to Ton Sai Bay. There are cliffs from 6 to 16 m that are ideal for cliff jumping due to the depth of water below. Organized tours can be found at Ton Sai. Please note that this is potentially dangerous and can cause injury to people including ear ruptures, and muscle/back injuries. Having said that, as long as you take it easy (not attempt weird flips on your first jump) and follow a simple feet-first technique, it is fairly safe and provides a surge of adrenaline that can only be topped by another, higher leap into the emerald water!

Buy

Supplies are brought in by boat, so most things are more expensive than on the mainland. However, there are a few shops that manufacture their goods on the island. Prices for commodities can vary widely between shops.

D's Books has a location on Ko Phi Phi and many others throughout southern Thailand. It is a well-respected book store.

Most of the items sold here are either made by local fishermen or they are brought to the island from Phuket. Rising commercialization and inflow of tourists throughout the year seems to be a big bonus for these locals. Prices told may exactly not be worth the item, but if you are a good talker you can bargain for a good price.

Learn

Rock Climbing Krabi region with its specific landscape is ideal for learning rock climbing, there are lots of different courses for beginners – advanced. The courses available range from just half a day to three whole days in length. All instructors are properly qualified and well-experienced. There are at least ten rock climbing schools in Rai Leh and Ton Sai, and several more on Ko Phi Phi (As of June 2016, all climbing shops/schools on Ko Phi Phi are closed or out of business. Please update this last note if you can verify that any new shops open).

Diving With its crystal clear water, colourful coral and huge diversity of marine life, Phi Phi is a must-go for all those interested in diving. There are courses for anyone, regardless to whether they are near-on experts or complete beginners. Beginner courses are on offer from a range of dive centres, with more advance PADI Open Water courses taking up to three to four days to complete. Koh Phi Phi has excellent visibility with average underwater visibility ranging from 10m to 15m. Local weather, currents and tides can impact visibility.

Kiteboarding Phi Phi island offers excellent conditions for learning kiteboarding. There are beaches on all sides of the island so any wind direction is suitable. There is only one school on the island and they provide IKO beginner courses as well as advanced lessons. Tours are also provided to nearby islands.

Thai Cooking There are a number of places around the island offering Thai Cooking Classes.

Eat

In general, Southern Thai food is renowned for its spiciness. Much of the cuisine has its origins in Malay, Indonesian and Indian food. Favourite dishes from the south include Indian-style Muslim curry (massaman), rice noodles in fish curry sauce (Khanom Jeen) and chicken with yellow rice.

Food on Ko Phi Phi is extremely varied, given the diminutive size of the island, but is not as spectacular as it generally is in Thailand, because most ingredients have to be brought in by boat from the mainland. Reasonably priced and tasty seafood is obviously what most tourists long for when visiting a coastal province like Krabi. In this connection, the wing shell is Krabi's famous dish and is eaten with a spicy dip. In addition, stirred fried Spotted Babylon, which is found in mangrove forests, with chillies and basil, is also famous. This dish is common in Krabi's restaurants.

- ✓ Calamero Resto - The usual suspects are served in this simple yet quality restaurant. A wide selection of breakfast, fresh pasta, pizza, Thai food, sandwiches and more is complemented by fruit shakes, liqueurs and evening cocktails. And the best "fried ice-cream". All food is clean, good, and reasonably priced.

- ✓ Cosmic - Italian restaurant - has two outlets on the island and serves pizza. All pizzas cost 150 baht, all Thai dishes with rice cost 80 baht.

- ✓ Mr. Tee's - When you come off the ferry, veer slightly left and you find yourself on an alley covered by tarps, with small Thai restaurants. You'll notice a lot of locals eating in this alley. The second booth on your left is Mr. Tee's. There's a signboard showing "Mr. Tee's" but its facing the other direction. They tend to be forgetful but the food is good, cheap, and spicy. There's a shop just opposite "Mr. Tee's", their food is just as good.

- ✓ Only Noodles Pad Thai - Small shack at the end of the lane between Irish Pub and Harmony Travel. Run alone by a friendly lady, and serves only pad Thai, with rice noodles, glass noodles, yellow noodles. 80-90 baht for chicken/shrimp pad Thai.

- ✓ Pad Thai Restaurant - Friendly and fun, Pad Thai Restaurant serves great tourist-friendly Thai food behind PP Island Village Resort. Many hotel guests eat better food there each night for 1/3 the price. Hand made spring rolls are excellent as are the garlic pepper fish and fried squid, bought fresh daily from local fishermen. The restaurant is easily accessible from PP Island Village Resort. Exit the rear of the hotel, turn right and walk 50 m to Pad Thai on the left. The restaurant and PP Island Village are also accessible by walking 25 minutes from Laem Tong. The staff can provide for a free motorcycle ride back after dark You can also book diving and snorkelling trips here. Can be quite busy between 19:00-21:00.

✓ Papaya - one of the first restaurants rebuilt after the tsunami. A small green "shop" restaurant opposite the Reggae Bar and next door to Tiger Bar, run by the enthusiastic and friendly Mr Nod. Don't let the unprepossessing looks of the restaurant put you off - the food here is incredibly good and very good value. Serves authentic Thai food, hot and spicy as it should be, but the staff gauge the spiciness as percentages, with 100% being "Thai spicy". Among local expats living on the island, this place may be known as the place to get good cheap Thai food but it's no longer the cheapest. If you are looking for a personal sized portion with rice at a cheaper price, ask for your food to be "On Rice". Help yourself to the drinks in the fridge, which will be included on the bill, and check out the cat which lives in there. Note: Papaya opens around 17:00 and, in high season, is packed by 18:00-19:00. Go early if you're not prepared to wait!

- ✓ The Pirate's House - Great Indian and Western food, but the Thai food is not the greatest. A bit pricey, but nice and clean. Do not go during peak dinner times food will take up to an hour to reach your table. Be careful when you take a seat, it's very easy to hurt your knees on their heavy and impractical wooden tables.

- ✓ Tuk's BBQ - Located next to Reggae Bar, it's a street vendor offering a good BBQ, with most items costing 30 baht.

- ✓ Pa-Noi Thai food - Located in the middle of Panmanee market. Its hard to miss it with all good rating and comments on their wall. Reasonable price, clean and tasty Tong Yam.

Drink

Ton Sai Bay has a variety of night life; something for everyone's taste. Jazz, blues, and classics can be found playing at the leading hotels. Or, if it's romance you are after, you and your loved one can relax in one of the beach bars and sip a cocktail under the stars.

If everything is cool, the police usually allow bars to open until about 01:00 in town and 04:00 on the beach.

- ✓ Beach Bar - located in the tsunami wastelands and a good choice for those looking to have a quiet drink.

- ✓ Breakers - American/Aussie-style pub with huge wide screen LCD screens. Great food, big portions, and an extensive selection of spirits as well as draught beer and cider.

- ✓ Blanco Beach Bar - Blanco Dorm room and beach bar. Western kitchen and fantastic views and party atmosphere.

- Carlitos Bar - relaxed drinks on the beach served by amiable staffers. During the winter months this place is full of Scandinavian party-goers. Most of the service staff this time of year is over on extended holiday from Sweden so expect a lot of beautiful tanned blonds to be walking around.

- Carpe Diem - Nice, relaxing beach chill out bar. Staff used to be notoriously bad, but these have recently been replaced with better staff.

- Deaf Gecko - Chilled beach bar on Nice Beach. Great music, fantastic staff, and quiet beach. Fresh fruit shakes, daiquiris, and loads of Leo beer. Open 17:00-01:00 nightly.

- ✓ Deco Bar - Excellent bar with chill music located above Phi Phi Scuba Dive Centre on the main road from the pier. Nightly specials & happy hour(s) with 100 baht mixed drinks, 50 baht beers and shisha/water pipes available. Try the spicy Thai mojito. Open 19:00-01:00 nightly.

- ✓ Hippies Bar - The original hippies has returned. Near the original location on the Tonsai Bay side, the same staff, great music, cocktails and nightly fire shows!

- ✓ Ibiza Bar - one of the best beach dance bars. A live music band, playing classic rock and roll hits, is a great feature as well. Don't miss the fire shows every night and great dancing and fun games.

- ✓ Mojito Bar - great cocktail bar with fantastic views and the friendliest staff. At Viewpoint Resort.

- ✓ Reggae Bar - popular place that organizes mock muay Thai fights most nights. If you are there at the right time you can even join in. They invite tourists, usually drunk, to get into the ring geared up and to beat on each other for a few rounds for a couple of free buckets.

- ✓ Rolling Stoned Bar - Great rock music with a live band during high season and at other times of the year. They also have four pool tables and is a one of the more popular bars on the island.

- ✓ Sports Bar (สปอร์ตซ บาร์) - Small English-style bar with a pool table and good pub food. For some great English-style meat pies Sports Bar is the place.

✓ Stockhome Syndrome bar located in the centre of town is a popular spot for all tourists, hosting the best music, beer pong tables, pool table and great drink offers on TWO floors, a great way to start your nights!!

✓ Tia and Millie Sunflower Bar - on Lohdalum Bay, a nautically-themed beach bar with and "ark" and longtail-bar, pool table, and laid-back beach seating. A great place to watch the often spectacular sunsets.

✓ Woody's Bar is just a liquor store, but they have a few tables out front. Its close to Apache. The staff are funny, and the Beatles music is often playing. Nice place to get a

180 baht bucket to walk around on the beach with.

Sleep

Accommodation is relatively expensive. Doubles range from 400 baht (fan only, with AC it starts at 600 baht) up into the thousands the closer you get to the beach front. If you are on a budget expect to work hard to find a decent price for a private room. Dorm rooms can be found for around 250-300 baht (AC included, shared shower and washroom). If you get really desperate, a couple of places rent out tents for about 200–300 baht. One thing to note, prices are double during the high season which runs from Oct-Nov until May. Other times of year you can find relatively cheap accommodation in the 200-300 baht range.

To have the best choice of accommodation, arrive in Phi Phi just before the Full Moon Party, when most people will be on Ko Pha Ngan. Since a lot of people move from Pha Ngan to Phi Phi after the party, accommodation may be very hard to find on Phi Phi around this time. It is not uncommon to see people arrive on the morning ferry only to leave on the afternoon one because they have been unsuccessful in finding accommodation.

Backpackers need only to look further east on the main street for relatively cheap accommodation. Certain guest houses have dorms, and some have reputations for being good sources of camaraderie and parties. Compare all the dorms. All are different.

Krabi Travel Destination, Thailand

- ✓ Paradise Dorm : THB 250 price for Feb, 2018. Nice air-con dorm, clean and close to pier. Its located next to nightclub Stockholm Syndrome.

- ✓ Blanco Dorm Room, . Cheap and clean dorm rooms directly on the beach. 3 styles to choose from. Restaurant and beach bar

- ✓ Chaokoh Phi Phi Lodge Resort, situated on Ton Sai Bay just ten minutes by walking to the pier. Nice with both fan and air-conditioned rooms near the beach for 1,200-3,500 baht.

- ✓ Holiday Inn Resort, . A great place to get away for couples and families. It is expensive by Thai standards. There are no clubs or bars in the area, and to get to any clubs or bars is by a 45 minute longtail boat ride. There are 4 resorts clustered on one beach. The cost in 2009 was USD$60/night garden bungalows, 3,000 baht sea view, USD$140/night beach front. Food at the resort is expensive, but there are two independent restaurants nearby. On the long-tail boat journey back from visiting Ko Phi Phi Leh it's recommended to stop at Ton Sai Bay for provisions as it's 1/3rd the price.

- ✓ Kinnaree House, . Rooms with private bathroom, twin or double bed for 1,000-2,000 baht. At the centre of Ko Phi Phi.

- ✓ Long Beach Resort a hotel with backpacker dorms located within the resort.

- ✓ Oasis Guest house. Nice fan rooms with clean shared bathrooms for 500 baht. Close to bars/restaurants but the noise doesn't make it to the rooms. Prices are simple, no negotiating, but good prices on rooms, tour packages, and travel to mainland. 500 baht.

✓ Phi Phi Andaman Legacy located on Ton Sai Bay and after guests get off the boat, about 7-10 minutes by walk straight on the beach side. Price ranges between 2,000-5,000 baht.

✓ PP Banyan Villa, situated on Ton Sai beach, 200 m from the main pier. Price: 2,000-5,200 baht including breakfast.

✓ PP Casita, situated in Loh Dalum 5 minutes by walking to the beach and 10 minutes from Ton Sai. Room rate are 1,500-4,000 baht.

✓ PP Charlie Beach Resort, situated on Loh Dalum Bay, Phi Phi Don. Price ranges between 1,500-2,500 baht. 100 m from the market, the Ton Sai pier, banks, and food shops.

✓ PP Erawan Palms Resort is a luxury beach resort with Thai island style accommodation, located on Leamtong Beach (cape of God), the northernmost beach on Phi Phi Don. Price ranges between 3,000-9,000 baht. Swimming pool overlooks the white powdery sand beach and emerald blue ocean.

✓ Phi Phi Hill Resort Long Beach (Had Yao) Great budget bungalows. As the name suggests, expect to take plenty of stairs to and from the beach (though there is a pulley system for your luggage). Sunrise bungalows 700-750 baht (fan) and Sunset bungalows 1,200-2,000 baht (fan or air-con, with breakfast).

- ✓ PP Island Cabana, Luxury hotel in Tonsai Bay, prime location closest to the main pier with spacious and large swimming pool. Price ranges between 2,800-20,000 baht.

- ✓ PP Island Resort, . A good place for honeymooners. Expensive. Some staff don't speak English. No pier when you arrive, so if it's low tide, you have to literally step into the ocean, walk up to the beach, to the resort - they raft your luggage in and out. starting from 4,700 baht.

- ✓ Phi Phi Lagoon Resort, (15 min by longtail from Ton Sai Bay to Loh Bagao or Loh Lana Bay), +66 75 623239 +66 84 8898225, . checkin: early; checkout: late. Remoteness personified. This is one of the best get-away family bungalow complexes on the island. It is not even easy to get there as you have to take a taxi boat after you arrive at the main pier. Amid coconut orchards, the resort offers comfortable but simple accommodation. No discos or loud music at night. The air conditioned bungalows will make your Robinson Crusoe on Pandora experience worthwhile. Daily fishing trips and BBQ parties with he owner of the resort is a special touch. Nearest hotel to the beautiful secluded beach at Nui Bay. 2,500 baht).

- ✓ Phi Phi Natural Resort situated in Laem Tong, the northernmost of Phi Phi islands. Price ranges between 2,500-8,500 baht. Public ferries from Krabi or Phuket to the resort are available. Accommodation is set amidst lush surroundings and the beach is just a short stroll from your cottage.

- ✓ PP Palm Tree situated at the heart of Phi Phi. Luxury, modern hotel with pool access. Price ranges between 4,000-8,500 baht including daily breakfast.

- ✓ Phi Phi Rimlay. Very nice air conditioned rooms near the beach for 800 baht.

- ✓ PP Viewpoint, . Wide variety of rooms from bungalows with fans to air-con with mini-bar, all with awesome views of the bay. Pool, full service dining, two bars, kayak rentals, diving lessons, and a private trail to the viewpoint. Poor food quality and the bill might be higher than listed on menu.

- ✓ Pongpan House a cheap guest house, located near Loh Dalum beach, the center of Ko Phi Phi. Prices range between 1,000-1,500 baht.

- ✓ The Rock Backpacker, +66 75 601021. Clean and friendly place and excellent for meeting up with other tourists. Costs are 200 baht dorm beds, 300 baht really tiny singles and a few 500 baht doubles (prices double during high season).

- ✓ View Garden Resort. Rooms with bathroom, double bed, and shared balcony for 300 baht.

- ✓ Viking Natures Resort, Viking Beach (15 min walk from town or take a longtail between Maprao and Long Beach), +66 75 819399 +66 78 5819398, +66 81 9308866, . Private and shared bungalows with good attention to detail. Safe, clean, and environmentally friendly with spectacular views.

Stay healthy

Ko Phi Phi has a couple of pharmacies and a hospital. For any bad illnesses, go back to Krabi or even better, Phuket.

Travelling responsibly

At the beaches and some bars some people may offer you to take your photograph with animals, even baby animals, in exchange for money. Please remember that the most likely way (and many times the only way) these babies were acquired were by poachers killing the mothers, or the entire family. Endorsing this practice only leads to more demand, and more killing. Moreover, some of the species used are endangered and protected under Thai law, which makes the possession and abuse of many of these animals illegal.

The Gibbon Rehabilitation Project is a sanctuary for former photo prop and pet gibbons, based in Phuket Island, they often receive Gibbons and report of more gibbons coming from Phi Phi, they have been working hard for the last decade to rehabilitate and reintroduce them into the wild, in the National Park by Bang Pae Waterfall, should you be interested in learning loads of information about these issues, you may visit their Education Centre inside the park.

The End

Printed in Great Britain
by Amazon